Classical Chinese for Everyone

A Guide for Absolute Beginners

Classical Chinese for Everyone

A Guide for Absolute Beginners

Bryan W. Van Norden

Hackett Publishing Company, Inc.
Indianapolis/Cambridge

Copyright © 2019 by Hackett Publishing Company, Inc.

22 21 20 19   1 2 3 4 5 6 7

For further information, please address
 Hackett Publishing Company, Inc.
 P.O. Box 44937
 Indianapolis, Indiana 46244-0937

 www.hackettpublishing.com

Cover design by Rick Todhunter
Interior design by E. L. Wilson
Composition by Aptara, Inc.

Library of Congress Cataloging-in-Publication Data

Names: Van Norden, Bryan W. (Bryan William), author.
    Title: Classical Chinese for everyone : a guide for absolute
    beginners / Bryan W. Van Norden.
Description: Indianapolis : Hackett Publishing Company,
    Inc., [2019] | Includes bibliographical references.
Identifiers: LCCN 2019010488 | ISBN 9781624668227 (cloth)
    | ISBN 9781624668210 (paperback)
Subjects: LCSH: Chinese language—Textbooks for foreign
    speakers—English.
Classification: LCC PL1129.E5 V36 2019 | DDC
    495.182/421—dc23
LC record available at https://lccn.loc.gov/2019010488

Contents

Preface

This book is designed to introduce Classical Chinese to students with no previous exposure to Modern Chinese. This differs from the approach used in most textbooks, which assumes you already have studied Chinese for at least a couple of years. (Some of these books also seem to assume that you plan on being a Sinologist and already have a master's degree in linguistics!)

I started studying Classical Chinese as an undergraduate (with Nathan Sivin at the University of Pennsylvania), after completing three years of Modern Chinese (studying under Victor Mair and the late A. Ronald Walton, among others). I continued my study as a graduate student in philosophy at Stanford, and translation has been an important part of my research and publications ever since. However, I learned from my teacher, the late David S. Nivison, that it is possible to teach Classical Chinese to students with no previous exposure to the language; he routinely included language instruction as part of his introductory course on ancient Chinese philosophy. Later, I was one of the founders of the Department of Chinese and Japanese at Vassar College, and I offered our first course in Classical Chinese. In the first years of the program, we simply did not have enough students to make two years of Modern Chinese a requirement for Classical Chinese. Consequently, I wrote the first draft of this textbook for our students. The Department of Chinese and Japanese at Vassar has flourished, and I now use Paul Rouzer's *A New Practical Primer of Literary Chinese* to teach students who have already learned Modern Chinese.

I still got some use out of my old textbook, though, sending PDFs to Western-trained philosophers and interested amateurs when they asked for a recommendation for a text to help them learn at least a little of the language of the classics of Confucianism and Daoism. On a whim, I submitted the manuscript to my editor at Hackett Publishing Company, Rick Todhunter, and he reported that there is a real hunger for a book like this.

So I owe a debt to my own teachers, to my students, and to my colleagues at Vassar, all of whom were essential for the eventual completion of this book. I am also grateful to my colleagues at Yale-NUS College, Scott Cook and Jing Hu, for assistance on some technical issues. Justin Tiwald and four anonymous referees also provided invaluable feedback and corrections to earlier drafts. Rick Todhunter has been very encouraging of this project from the beginning. In addition, Hackett's production director, Liz Wilson, and this book's copyeditor, Shannon Cunningham, and its proofreader, Leslie Connor, have made me sound much more articulate than I am. None of these people is responsible for my mistakes, of course.

Introduction

Classical Chinese is the form of Chinese that was written in the period between roughly 500 BCE and 220 CE. It is the language of classical Confucianism and Daoism. This book is designed to introduce you to the fundamentals of Classical Chinese grammar, some basic vocabulary, and fundamental skills in using a dictionary and classical commentaries. After reading this book, you will still have a lot to learn. However, you should be ready to continue learning from a more conventional textbook. In addition, with perseverance and the help of a good grammar and dictionary, you will be able to work your way through a few elementary Chinese texts on your own.

Two aspects of this book are distinctive. First, most other textbooks of Classical Chinese assume that you have already completed at least two years of Modern Chinese or Japanese. However, this textbook assumes no previous familiarity with the Chinese or Japanese spoken or written languages. Second, from the very first lesson, this book teaches you using selections from actual Chinese philosophical texts. These include readings from the sayings of Confucius, Laozi (the legendary founder of Daoism), and some Tang dynasty poetry. In three lessons I edited the text slightly, but all of the other readings are complete, and none of the readings are artificial or dumbed down.

Classical Chinese is a style of Literary Chinese, the written language used by the educated in China for approximately 2,500 years.[1] It was also adopted as the literary language of premodern Korea, Japan, and Vietnam. In a way, Literary Chinese played a role in East Asia similar to Latin in the West. Latin and Literary Chinese were originally the written form

---

1. There is also an earlier pre-Classical language (called Old Chinese or Archaic Chinese) that we know from inscriptions on artifacts and the older portions of works like the *Classic of Odes* (詩經 Shījīng) and the *Classic of Documents* (書經 Shūjīng), which were already ancient by the time of Confucius.

of the language spoken natively by a particular group of people. However, the ordinary vernacular language evolved into various spoken dialects, and Latin and Literary Chinese became the common written languages of the educated elites. In the West, books were first printed using vernacular English, German, etc. during the Protestant Reformation (beginning in the sixteenth century), but educated people were expected to know Latin until the beginning of the twentieth century. In China, almost all texts were printed in Literary Chinese until the New Culture movement of the early twentieth century.

1. The Five Types of Chinese Characters

Everyone knows that there is something distinctive about the Chinese writing system, but there is considerable ignorance and confusion about how that writing system works.[2] Almost two thousand years ago, the Chinese lexicographer 許慎 Xǔ Shèn noted that there are five kinds of Chinese characters: pictograms, simple ideograms, compound ideograms, loan characters, and semantic-phonetic compounds.[3] We can illustrate four of these five types using symbols that are familiar to contemporary English readers.

---

2. Sections 1–3 of this Introduction are reprinted, with modifications, from Bryan W. Van Norden, *Introduction to Classical Chinese Philosophy* (Indianapolis: Hackett Publishing, 2011), Appendix B, 235–47.

3. Nerd note: In Chinese, these are known as 象形字 xiàngxíngzì (pictograms), 指事字 zhǐshìzì (simple ideograms), 會意字 huìyìzì (compound ideograms), 形聲字 xíngshēngzì (semantic-phonetic compounds, which are also referred to as 諧聲字 xiéshēngzì), and 假借字 jiǎjièzì (phonetic loans). Xǔ Shèn explained his system in his 說文解字 Shuōwén jiězì, *Explanation of Simple Characters and Analysis of Complex Characters*, from about 100 CE. Xǔ Shèn also identified a sixth type of character, but there is no consensus about what he thought the defining feature of this type is, so people generally ignore it.

Pictograms were originally drawings of something:

As these examples illustrate, the pictures are usually stylized, sometimes to the point of being purely conventional. The image on the far right looks nothing like a real human heart, but children are taught in kindergarten that it is a "picture" of a heart. In addition, the relationship between the picture's meaning and what it depicts has a large element of conventionality. The middle symbol means "smoking permitted here," but our culture could equally well have decided that it means "tobacco sold here" or "warning, flammable materials present." So pictograms are pictures of something, but their meaning is still determined to a great extent by social convention.

Simple ideograms are characters whose structure suggests their meaning, but which were not pictures of anything concrete:

The simple ideogram on the far left means "five," but it is not a picture, because the number five is an abstract entity, so there could not be a picture of it. As with pictograms, there is an element of conventionality in the meanings of simple ideograms. The middle symbol is posted on roads and means "U-turn allowed," but we as a society could have decided that it means "watch out for falling balls" and posted it on golf courses or baseball parks.

Compound ideograms are characters with two or more meaningful components that in conjunction suggest the meaning of the composite symbol:

Notice that the components of the compound ideogram on the left are themselves ideograms. However, the compound ideogram in the middle has one component that is a pictogram and one that is an ideogram. The compound ideogram on the far right has two components that are pictograms. In general, the components of a compound ideogram do not have to be ideograms themselves. All that is necessary is that the conjunction of meaningful symbols suggests the meaning of the whole.

The previous three types of characters categorize them according to the way in which they are *created*. The next category, phonetic loans, includes characters that already exist but that are *recycled* to represent a new meaning. Simply put, a phonetic loan is a rebus. If you are not familiar with that term, consider the following "sentence":

It means, "I love you." But how does it get this meaning? Left to right, the symbols are a pictogram of an eye (from the seal on the back of the US dollar bill), a pictogram of a human heart, and a pictogram of a hand pointing at the reader. The eye pictogram does not stand for a human eye here, of course. Instead, it stands for a word that sounds the same as "eye" in English: "I." This is how phonetic loans work: they borrow pre-existing symbols that already have a word associated with them and use them to represent *different* words that *sound* the same.

Most people, if they have any preconceptions about Chinese characters, seem to think that they all work like pictograms or ideograms. In fact, only a small percentage of Chinese characters are either pictograms or ideograms. Almost all Chinese characters (97 percent) belong to the fifth group of characters: semantic-phonetic compounds. As we have seen, there are examples of pictograms, ideograms, and even phonetic loans that will be familiar to English readers. However, semantic-phonetic compounds are a little harder to illustrate. Consider the following sentence:

The first symbol in the above sentence is a pictogram of an eye, being used as a phonetic loan for "I." The third symbol is still a pictogram for "you." But what is the eye pictogram doing in its second occurrence? It means "see." So the sentence means "I see you." Perhaps you guessed this immediately, but if there were lots of pictograms in common use and they had different meanings, sometimes used as phonetic loans and other times pictograms proper, you could easily get confused. So we might start to distinguish one use of a symbol from another by providing an additional hint:

The first symbol is now a semantic-phonetic compound. The eye pictogram in the first symbol is the phonetic component: it tells us what the pronunciation of the character is. The man pictogram in the first symbol is the semantic component: it gives you a hint about what the meaning of the symbol is. If we were properly trained in reading this written language, we would immediately read the above sentence as "I see you." Now consider the following pictogram of a handsaw:

Suppose we combine this symbol with the eye symbol, producing the semantic-phonetic compound in the middle of the sentence below:

This sentence would mean "I saw you." The first two symbols in this sentence are both semantic-phonetic compounds, in which one part gives you a hint about the pronunciation of the symbol and one part gives you a hint about the meaning. Chinese semantic-phonetic compounds work the same way.

Now that we understand the five types of Chinese characters, let's look at some actual examples. Pictograms, once again, are stylized pictures that have a meaning that is conventionally connected to what they depict:

日　月　女　子

Try to guess what these four characters are pictures of, and then look at the footnote for the answer.[4] If you guessed even one of them correctly, you have done as well as any student has ever done in the thirty years that I have been using this example. In all likelihood, you couldn't guess any of them. As I stressed before, pictograms are highly stylized symbols whose meaning is not transparent.

---

4. Believe it or not, these are (from left to right) pictograms of the sun, the moon, a woman, and a child.

Simple ideograms, you will recall, are characters whose structure suggests their meaning but which are not pictures of anything. Simple ideograms are quite rare in Chinese, but here are some examples:

一　二　三　上　下

You might be able to guess the meanings of the first three symbols, especially when you see them written side by side like this. The fourth and the fifth characters are less transparent, though.[5]

Compound ideograms are characters with two parts, each of which has a meaning on its own, which suggests the meaning of the whole character when they are brought into conjunction:

明　好

You now know the meanings of the components of each of these two compound ideograms. (Look back under the examples of pictograms if you have forgotten.) Based on the components, try to guess the meaning of each of these compound ideograms before looking at the footnote.[6]

Semantic-phonetic compounds have one part that hints at the meaning of the character (the semantic component) and one part that hints at the pronunciation (the phonetic component). For example, the pictogram 門 depicts a gate and is pronounced mén, but it occurs as the phonetic component in the following semantic-phonetic compounds:

---

5. From left to right, these are the simple ideograms for the numbers one, two, three, above, and below. (And, no, the character for "four" is not what you would guess.)

6. The compound ideogram on the left means "bright" (suggested by the combined brightness of the sun, 日, and the moon, 月), while the one on the right means (in Classical Chinese) "to be fond of" (suggested by a woman, 女, holding her child, 子). The original form of 明 may have shown a window and the moon, which would also be a compound ideogram, but with different components.

問 wèn, "to ask" (the semantic component is 口, "mouth")

聞 wén, "to hear" (the semantic component is 耳, "ear")

們 men (pluralizing suffix in Modern Chinese; the semantic component is 亻, "person")

悶 mèn, "to be sad" (the semantic component is 忄, "heart")

Not all phonetic components are as useful as these. The pronunciations of Chinese characters have changed greatly over time, so a phonetic element that was helpful when the character was first created two thousand years or more ago may be almost useless today. However, it is good to get into the habit of recognizing phonetic elements in characters, because they do often aid in memorization.

Phonetic loan characters are originally created in one of the four previous ways: pictograms, simple ideograms, compound ideograms, or semantic-phonetic compounds. But they are recycled to represent different words that sound the same as (or similar to) the words that they originally represented. For example, the character 來 was originally a pictogram of wheat. It was borrowed to represent the homophone meaning "to come." Similarly, the character 其 was originally a pictogram of a basket, but it was borrowed to represent the meanings "his," "her," "its," or "their." The phonetic loan principle is very important in explaining the origin of many characters. In addition, we have learned from ancient manuscripts discovered in excavated tombs that it was once extremely common for scribes to substitute homophonous characters for one another.

In summary, almost all Chinese characters (again, about 97 percent) are semantic-phonetic compounds, in which part of the character gives a hint about the meaning and part gives a hint about the pronunciation. In addition, a handful of characters are created as pictograms, simple ideograms, or complex ideograms—in which there is a conventional connection between the structure of the character and its meaning. Finally, some characters that are created in one of the preceding ways are used to represent homophones in the spoken language.

I have been stressing two things: the conventionality of the meaning of Chinese characters and their strong connection with the spoken language. I have been doing this in order to inoculate you against what is sometimes called "the ideographic myth," the mistaken belief that Chinese characters somehow directly represent ideas or meanings, without conventions or connections to the spoken language. One extreme illustration of the ideographic myth is provided by the 1960 science fiction film *12 to the Moon*. In this film, an international crew of astronauts receives a video transmission from space aliens that is written in what the astronauts describe as "hieroglyphs." The Japanese crewmember helps out by sight-translating the alien script.[7] The "logic" here is apparently that *kanji* (the Chinese characters used in written Japanese) are hieroglyphs, and both are pictures, and as such they have intrinsic meaning that can be understood by anyone familiar with any picture-language. I hope that, even before reading this book, you would roll your eyes at this scene, but you are guilty of a similar misconception if you think that Chinese characters are all pictures, or have no connection with spoken words. So remember: characters usually provide some phonetic information, and even if you know exactly what the structure of a Chinese character is, you will not necessarily know what it means. Like a word in any language, written or spoken, to know the meaning of a character you must know how it is used.

How many characters are there? This question is not as easy to answer as it might seem, because the answer depends on whether we count variant forms of the same character (some of them extremely obscure) and whether we count characters that are now completely obsolete. (Is the British "civilisation" a different word from the American "civilization"?

---

7. Nerd note: Part of this scene is shown in the trailer for the film, which can be found on YouTube. If you find the complete film, the relevant scene starts around 45 minutes in. By the way, Egyptian hieroglyphs are not all pictograms either. Many of them are phonetic loans.

Is Shakespeare's "fardels" still an English word?) The larger Chinese dictionaries that aim at being comprehensive have sixty thousand characters or more. But don't despair: the three thousand most common characters include 99 percent of all characters in use in contemporary Chinese documents. In addition, the eight thousand characters in Kroll's *Student's Dictionary of Classical and Medieval Chinese* include almost every character you are likely to run across in the most commonly read premodern documents.

There have been various proposals for reforming or simplifying the Chinese written language. In the 1950s, the government of the People's Republic of China (PRC) introduced a set of simplified characters. These characters are often based on the handwritten cursive style of characters that have been used for centuries when writing informally. So, for example, 習, "to practice," was simplified to 习, and 門, "gate," was simplified to 门. Not all characters have a simplified form; in those cases, people still use the "long" or "traditional" form.[8] Most contemporary Chinese language programs in the United States teach the simplified forms. However, the traditional forms are often used by Chinese outside the PRC, including the Republic of China (ROC on Taiwan). In addition, well-educated people in the PRC also recognize the long-form characters.

People sometimes have very passionate views about the choice to use simplified or long forms. (I once got yelled at by someone at a conference in mainland China for including some traditional characters in the printed version of my talk.) In any case, in this book we will use primarily the long forms of the characters, although I will supply the simplified form of a character in parentheses (when there is one) in the vocabulary list for each lesson.

---

8. Nerd note: In Chinese, "simplified character" is jiǎntǐzì and is written (with the simplified form in parentheses) 簡體字 (简体字). "Long form" or "traditional" characters are called 繁體字 (繁体字) fántǐzì.

2. Spoken Chinese

The sounds of Chinese words and characters can be written with a romanization system, which is a method of writing a spoken language using the letters of the Roman alphabet. The standard phonetic system for Mandarin Chinese today is Pinyin, which is the one used by the PRC, the United Nations, US news organizations, and almost all contemporary Chinese language textbooks. Prior to the development of Pinyin, Wade-Giles was the standard romanization system. Many older books, articles, and reference works use Wade-Giles, so it is convenient to know if you are really serious about Sinological research. You can recognize a Wade-Giles romanization by the frequent use of apostrophes and hyphens. For example, "Kongzi" (Confucius) in Pinyin is "K'ung-tzu" in Wade-Giles. Pinyin is also distinctive because it begins words with letter combinations that do not occur in English. For example, "qian" and "zhou" are Pinyin romanizations, corresponding to "ch'ien" and "chou" in Wade-Giles.

Two aspects of spoken Chinese make it especially challenging: dialects and tones. The dialects of Chinese are as different from one another as are French, Spanish, and Italian. Fortunately, everyone in China who has graduated from high school can speak what we call the Mandarin dialect, even though they may have been raised speaking another dialect and use that in their home village.[9] We do not know exactly how spoken Chinese sounded in the time of Confucius, so it is standard to pronounce the classical texts in whatever contemporary dialect you speak.

In Modern Chinese, the same set of phonemes (basic sounds) will be a different word depending on the tone with which they are pronounced. Mandarin has four tones (or five, if you count the absence of a tone as a

---

9. Nerd note: Mandarin is called 普通話 (普通话) pǔtōnghuà, "common speech," in the PRC and 國語 (国语) guóyǔ, the "national language," in the Republic of China (ROC) in Taiwan. You can also just say 中國話 (中国话) zhōngguóhuà, "Chinese speech," and people will assume you mean the Mandarin dialect.

tone). Nowadays, tones are usually represented with accent marks over the vowels. So (to use the example found in almost every textbook), *ma* can have five different meanings:

> mā 媽, n., "mom" (semantic-phonetic compound;
>   semantic element is 女, "woman")
> má 麻, n., "hemp" (pictogram of plants drying in a shed)
> mǎ 馬, n., "horse" (pictogram of a horse)
> mà 罵, t.v., "to scold" (semantic-phonetic compound;
>   semantic element is a double 口, "mouth")
> ma 嗎, g.p. (sentence-final particle marking a question)
>   (semantic-phonetic compound; semantic element is 口,
>   "mouth")

Notice that 馬, the pictogram of a horse, occurs as the phonetic element in three of the other characters. The following is a rough approximation of the tones. The first tone is high and level, similar to the way you would say, "g" if a music teacher said, "Give me a 'g.'" The second tone rises up, as if you were saying, "Huh?" The third tone dips down slightly, then rises up, like an old teacher answering a knock on the door by saying, "Yeeeeeeeees?" The fourth tone goes down, like disciplining a naughty dog: "No!"

I am not going to try to teach you how to pronounce Chinese in this textbook, because the best way to learn is by hearing and copying someone who is a native speaker. However, here are some free resources that give you paradigms of how to pronounce the syllables of Modern Mandarin:

- "Mandarin Chinese Pinyin Chart with Audio," *Yabla*, https://chinese.yabla.com/chinese-pinyin-chart.php (accessed February 6, 2019). This chart displays all the syllables in Mandarin Chinese. When you click on a syllable, you get a menu that lets you select the tone in which to hear it pronounced.
- "Mandarin Chinese Pinyin Chart," *DigMandarin*, https://www.digmandarin.com/chinese-pinyin-chart (accessed February 6, 2019). Similar to the preceding but with the syllables drawn out

more (which makes them easier to hear, but is less faithful to actual speech).

- "Say It Right," *Chinesepod*, https://chinesepod.com/tools/pronunciation (accessed February 6, 2019). This is a series of lessons explaining in detail Pinyin pronunciation. If you have the patience, this is actually a good way to learn pronunciation.
- Pleco Software, *Pleco Chinese Dictionary*, https://www.pleco.com/ (accessed February 6, 2019). The basic version of this app is available for both iOS and Android free of charge. It includes pronunciations (read in either a male or female voice) for each character and provides a variety of ways to look up characters, including by Pinyin romanization or by the "radical" (explained in the next section). Best of all, you can just write a character with your finger on the screen to look it up. You can pay for various add-ons, including Kroll's *Student's Dictionary of Classical and Medieval Chinese* (discussed below).

3. Dictionaries and Radicals

By this point you might be wondering how to look up a character in a Chinese dictionary. Some contemporary dictionaries are organized phonetically and alphabetized according to Pinyin romanization. But what if you don't already know how to pronounce a character? Most Chinese dictionaries have a finding list that follows the famous *Kang Xi Dictionary* (康熙字典 Kāng Xī Zìdiǎn, published 1716 CE) in organizing characters according to 214 radicals (部首 bù shǒu). In principle, every Chinese character has at least one radical in it, or the character is itself a radical. So if you encounter a character that you do not recognize, you first take a guess about what its radical is. Usually the radical is fairly easy to spot, but sometimes there is more than one radical, and other times the radical may be obscure. Next, count the number of "strokes" in the character in addition to the radical, where a stroke is defined by when you would lift up the brush or pen in order to draw the next line. With this information, go to the part of the dictionary that lists all the characters with that radical plus that many additional strokes. There will typically be a number of characters fitting this description, so you go down the list until you find the character you are looking for.

A traditional dictionary whose main entries are organized by radicals will usually also have an index that allows you to find a character by its pronunciation, and another index organized by the total number of strokes in the character. This last system works well for short lists of characters (like in the glossary of this book), but finding a character by its strokes in a full dictionary is a last resort, as there are (for example) about two hundred characters with six strokes in even a basic dictionary.

See the end of section 6 in this Introduction for recommendations for dictionaries of Classical Chinese.

4. A Note on Japanese

Someone once said to me: "I hear you're an expert on China. I'm going to Tokyo next week. Any advice?" I explained, as gently as I could, that China and Japan are not the same country. Perhaps you wouldn't make the same mistake, but people often fail to realize just how different the Chinese and Japanese languages are. In fact, spoken Chinese and Japanese are not merely distinct languages: they are in completely different language families. This means that spoken English is more closely related historically and structurally to Hindi than Japanese is to Chinese. For example, Japanese is a highly inflected language, where endings on verbs and nouns change to reflect tense, politeness level, etc. Chinese is uninflected; it does by context or grammatical particles what languages like Japanese and English do with inflections. This is why it is so utterly amazing that, more than a thousand years ago, the Japanese adopted the Chinese writing system.

Consider this example of how one verb functions differently in English, Japanese, and Chinese:

English	Japanese	Chinese
to drink	nomu	yǐn
drink	nomimasu	yǐn
drank	nomimashita	yǐn
not drink	nomimasen	bù yǐn
can drink	nomeru	huì yǐn
Drink!	Nominasai!	Yǐn ba!

As this example suggests, the same character can easily represent one verb in Chinese because the ending on the verb does not change, and grammatical function words can be represented by separate characters. However, characters do not work well for representing Japanese verbs, because they do not give you a way to express the changing inflections.

Traditional Japanese writers solved this problem by developing a two-track writing system. For centuries, high literature and official documents in Japanese were written in Chinese characters with Chinese grammar. Anyone who can read Literary Chinese can read these works written by Japanese authors. The same thing happened in Korea and Vietnam, which also have a rich, native literatures written in Literary Chinese.[10] In addition to writing in Chinese, Japanese authors also developed multiple phonetic scripts, derived from stylized forms of characters but used to represent syllables in Japanese. These latter scripts were used to transcribe diaries, novels, or other works using Japanese words and syntax. Eventually, a hybrid script developed that combined Chinese characters (called *kanji* in Japanese) to represent some common nouns and the stems of verbs along with two phonetic scripts (called *kana*) to represent verb endings, distinctive Japanese grammatical particles, and loanwords from Western languages.

---

10. Nerd note: I hate to admit it, but the Wikipedia page on "Kanbun" (漢文, the Japanese name for Chinese text) is actually the best introductory-level reading I know on Sino-Japanese, its various forms, and its writing conventions. See Wikipedia Contributors, "Kanbun," *Wikipedia, The Free Encyclopedia*, https://en.wikipedia.org/wiki/Kanbun (accessed February 6, 2019).

Here are the same examples from above, but with *kanji* and *kana*:

English	Japanese		Chinese
to drink	飲む		飲
drink	飲みます		飲
drank	飲みました		飲
not drink	飲みません		不飲
can drink	飲める		會飲
Drink!	飲みなさい!		飲吧!

Let's now look at how a simple sentence would be written differently in idiomatic Modern Chinese and Japanese:

I put the book on the table.
我把書放在桌子上。
私はテーブルの上に本を置きます。

In the Japanese sentence, テーブル are *katakana*, a syllabic script used to represent foreign names and loanwords, like "table" (*tēburu*). The following symbols are *hiragana* used to represent Japanese grammatical particles: は, の, に, を. The other *hiragana* represent the inflection of the verb: きます. Notice also that the characters 我 wǒ "I," 書 shū "book," and 放 fàng "to put" in the Chinese sentence are replaced respectively by the *kanji* 私 (*watakushi*), 本 (*hon*), and 置 (*oku*) in Japanese. (In Chinese, these characters mean "selfish" [read *sī*], "root" [*běn*], and "to install, to set up" [*zhì*].) The only character the two sentences have in common is 上, "top" (read *ue* in Japanese and shàng in Chinese).

In this book, I will sometimes note similarities between Chinese and Japanese, but keep in mind that these are often coincidental.

5. Writing Chinese Characters

When you learned to write the letters of the alphabet, your teachers didn't just show you what the letters look like and say, "Make something that looks like *that,* any way you can." Instead, they showed you *how* to write each letter, following a specific pattern. For example, in writing the letter "*a*," you (probably) learned to start writing it at the top, move your hand to the left and down until you finish the curve, then lift the pen up to go back to the top, before finishing the back of the letter with a straight line. You practiced this again and again, until it became so automatic that now you don't even think about doing it. In addition, you learned that the printed form of the letter, "*a*," is different from the handwritten form, "*a*," that there is a cursive form for writing quickly, a Gothic form that was used in some old documents and sometimes for stylistic reasons today, etc. Each of these styles of writing the letters of our alphabet has analogous styles in writing Chinese characters. The guides to writing characters that you will find in almost every book and website on the topic use "regular script," which is where you should start. But keep in mind that you will see in print and in Chinese calligraphy different forms of these characters.[11]

At the beginning, the most important thing to learn is how to write the "strokes," the lines and curves, that make up a Chinese character, and what order to write them in. In the Character List for each lesson, I give you the Pinyin romanization of each character. You can use that to look up the character in any of a number of guides to the proper stroke order for characters. For example, the ROC Ministry of Education has a website where you can look up an animation of the stroke order for the most common characters: http://stroke-order.learningweb.moe.edu.tw/pinyin.do (accessed February 6, 2019). There are also apps for this purpose, including a paid add-on for the *Pleco Chinese Dictionary* (discussed above). I'm old fashioned and prefer actual books. See the end of section 6 of this Introduction for recommendations.

---

11. Nerd note: The main styles of Chinese writing are regular script (楷書 kǎishū), semi-cursive script (行書 xíngshū, also called "running style"), cursive script (草書 cǎoshū, also called "grass style"), seal script (篆書 zhuànshū), and clerical script (隸書 lìshū). The first two are what you would guess they are like from their names. The third style, fully cursive script, is used primarily for artistic purposes and is often illegible to even native readers of Chinese. Seal script and clerical script are analogues to Carolingian and Gothic scripts (roughly).

The great Chinese calligrapher 王羲之 Wáng Xīzhī (303–361 CE) said that there are eight different kinds of strokes that make up all Chinese characters.[12] However, different teachers and texts give different lists. The following rules will guide you to draw the strokes in the correct way most of the time:

> Horizontal strokes go from left to right.
> Vertical strokes go from top to bottom.
> Curved or angled strokes go downhill (usually).
> Dots are small downward strokes.

By "curved," I mean any stroke that is not approximately straight; by "angled," I mean lines that are neither flat horizontal nor straight vertical. The main exception to these rules is a kind of angled stroke found in some characters that runs from lower left to upper right.

The order of strokes is usually

> First left-hand part of the character, then the right-hand part.
> First the top part, then the bottom part.
> First the outer part, then the inner part.
> When two strokes cross, first the horizontal stroke, then the vertical stroke.
> First the down and to the left stroke, then the down and to the right stroke.

I recommend that you get some paper intended for character practice that has columns with regular boxes. You can find this online and print it out, buy it in places where Chinese parents shop for their kids, or make your own. Write each new character at least fifty times. Learn to write a

---

12. Nerd note: These are the 橫 héng (horizontal stroke), 豎 shù (vertical stroke), 撇 piě (down and to the left), 捺 nà (down and to the right), 鉤 gōu (hook-shaped), 折 zhé (corner), 點 diǎn (dot), and 挑 tiǎo (lower left to upper right).

character using the correct stroke order, and with the strokes written in the right directions. Characters written correctly will look better, and it is hard to unlearn habits once you have ingrained them.

6. Introducing the Lessons

Each lesson in this textbook has four parts: (1) the readings, (2) the vocabulary, (3) the grammar notes, and (4) supplemental discussions.

(1) The readings are written in a traditional Chinese style: start in the upper right-hand corner of the page and read down the column; when you get to the bottom of the column, go to the next column to the left and read down again. The punctuation is also traditional, consisting only of a dot, 。 , which sometimes functions like a comma, sometimes like a period, and sometimes like some other mark of Western punctuation. (Most texts printed prior to the Qing dynasty, 1644–1911 CE, were not punctuated at all.)

(2) The vocabulary list gives the new characters introduced in each reading, as well as any old characters that are being used with new meanings. If the simplified form is significantly different from the long form, the simplified form is supplied in parentheses. After the character is its pronunciation in Pinyin romanization. (A handful of characters have more than one pronunciation, but usually only the pronunciation relevant to the reading is given.) Following the romanization is an abbreviation indicating the grammatical class of the word. (There is a complete list explaining these abbreviations at the end of this Introduction.) Then I give the meaning of the character as used in this lesson along with meanings introduced in earlier lessons. (Sometimes more than one meaning is given if the character is ambiguous, or if it helps to understand some related meanings of the word.) You should learn to recognize and write the long forms of these characters, pronounce them, and give any meanings you have learned for them.

(3) The grammar notes for a reading introduce the text from which the reading is taken (the first time it is used). They then explain the new grammatical constructions that are found in this reading. In every lesson,

I shall give you greatly simplified accounts of Chinese grammar. I will tell you what you need to know to understand the reading for the upcoming lesson (and maybe a *little* bit more). I do this because if I gave you a completely nuanced account of the use of every grammatical construction or particle at the moment I introduced it, you would almost certainly get lost in the details. (My "Nerd Notes" supply additional details and qualifications, and references to other works with more information.)

(4) The supplemental discussions after a lesson contain information about how Classical Chinese differs from Modern Chinese, or about historical and philosophical aspects of the text. There is also a glossary at the end of this book that includes every character and expression introduced in the lessons, organized by the number of strokes in the character (or in the first character in the expression).

My recommendation is that, for each lesson, you start with the vocabulary list and learn to recognize and pronounce the characters. Next, glance over the grammar notes (ignoring the "Nerd Notes" at first and just trying to get the gist of the grammar). Then try to understand the reading, without having the vocabulary list or the grammar notes in front of you. After you think you have understood the reading (or if you become hopelessly confused while trying to do the reading), review the vocabulary list and the grammar notes, to make sure you haven't missed anything.[13] You cannot reread or review too many times! In traditional China, kids (usually only upper-class boys, but some women were also very literate) would start reading Classical Chinese at age five, and repeat every sentence from the classics out loud at least fifty times to *begin with*, so you have a lot of catching up to do.

There are several other works that you will find extremely useful in your quest to learn Classical Chinese.

---

13. You can find translations of all of the philosophical texts in this book in Philip J. Ivanhoe and Bryan W. Van Norden, eds., *Readings in Classical Chinese Philosophy*, 2nd ed. (Indianapolis: Hackett Publishing, 2005). But don't use pre-existing translations as a substitute for trying to understand the text on your own. After all, translations frequently disagree.

Fuller, Michael A. *An Introduction to Literary Chinese.* Rev. ed. Harvard University Press, 2004. I have a slight preference for Rouzer's textbook (see below), but this is also a good textbook for students who already know Modern Chinese, or for you to continue with after you have finished the book you are reading now.

Hackett Publishing, support page for *Classical Chinese for Everyone,* https://www.hackettpublishing.com/chinese-for-everyone-support. The support page for this textbook will provide up-to-date links for relevant web resources, along with supplemental learning and teaching materials.

Harbaugh, Rick. *Chinese Characters: A Genealogy and Dictionary.* Yale University Press, 1999. This work gives you traditional etymologies of the characters, which are very helpful for memorizing the characters and for making small talk with people at parties. It is also available online at http://zhongwen.com/ (accessed February 6, 2019).[14]

Kroll, Paul W. *A Student's Dictionary of Classical and Medieval Chinese.* Rev. ed. Brill, 2017. This is, by far, the best Chinese-English dictionary for Classical Chinese. If you read it carefully, you will also find some wonderfully snarky comments about other dictionaries. This is available as a paid add-on to the *Pleco Chinese Dictionary* (discussed above).

McNaughton, William, and Jiageng Fang, *Reading and Writing Chinese.* 3rd ed. Tuttle Publishing, 2013. This and Teng, *Far East 3000* (see below), are two books that show you the proper stroke order to write the most common characters in Modern Chinese. Some of the characters in my lessons are not in these books, but those characters are composed of components that are in these books. You only need one of these two books.

Pulleyblank, Edwin G. *Outline of Classical Chinese Grammar.* UBC Press, 1996. This book is detailed and clear with lots of examples drawn from classical texts, and I will often cross-reference it in the "Nerd Notes" so you can look up more detailed explanations.

Rouzer, Paul. *A New Practical Primer of Literary Chinese.* Harvard University Asia Center, 2007. This is my favorite textbook for teaching

---

14. Nerd note: Harbaugh's etymologies are generally based on the dictionary of Xǔ Shèn, which we discussed above. This dictionary is very important historically. However, we are learning more about the history of Chinese characters all the time, so the traditional etymologies given by Xǔ Shèn (or Harbaugh) are often inaccurate.

students who already know Modern Chinese, or for you to continue with after you have finished the book you are reading now.

Sturgeon, Donald, ed. *Chinese Text Project*, https://ctext.org (accessed February 6, 2019). This is a wonderful resource that provides a searchable online database of some of the major works of Chinese philosophy, history, literature, and canonical classics. Every philosophical work found in this book is also available in full on the *Chinese Text Project*.

Teng Shou-hsin, ed. *The Far East 3000 Chinese Character Dictionary (Traditional Character Version)*. Far East Book Company, 2003. You can use this book or McNaughton and Fang (see above) to learn the proper stroke order for characters.

Van Norden, Bryan W. *Introduction to Classical Chinese Philosophy*. Hackett Publishing, 2011. This book will give you useful historical background along with readable summaries of the overall philosophies of the thinkers whom you will be reading below.

7. Abbreviations for Grammatical Classes

adv. = adverb (word that modifies a verb or adjective: "quickly," "slowly," "mutually," "in response")

conj. = conjunction (word that joins two phrases: "and," "or")

exp. = multiword expression or phrase

g.p. = grammatical particle (words that mark or transform the grammatical class of another word; inflections, prepositions, and auxiliary verbs do similar functions in English)

n. = noun (a word that refers to a thing; "mother," "son," "duke," "table," "righteousness")

prep. = preposition (a word that indicates a relationship between two nouns, or between a noun and a verb: "by," "with," "from," "of")

s.v. = stative verb (a verb that characterizes the quality of something: "are close," "is far," "will be tired")

t.v. = transitive verb (a verb that requires a noun to complete its sense: "hit [the ball]," "read [the book]")

v. = verb (special use verb not easy to classify as stative or transitive)

L e s s o n 1

1.1. Reading: *Analects* 17.2

習　子
相　曰
遠　。
也　性
。　相
　　近
　　也
　　。

1.2. Vocabulary

(Eight new characters)

子 zǐ n., Master (here refers to 孔子 Kǒngzǐ, who is better known in the West by the Latinization of his name, "Confucius")

曰 yuē v., to say (used to introduce a direct quotation)[1]

性 xìng n., nature (as in "human nature" or "the natures of humans")

相 xiāng adv., to each other

近 jìn s.v., to be close

也 yě g.p. (comes at end of sentences to mark nominal sentences; often indicates a generalization)

習 (习) xí n., practices

遠 or 遠 (远) yuǎn s.v., to be far

1.3. Grammar Notes

Stative Verbs, Adverbs, and Nominal Sentences

This reading is the complete text of *Analects* 17.2.[2] The *Analects* (known in Chinese as the 論語 (论语) Lúnyǔ, which probably means "Categorized

---

1. Nerd note: In a later lesson we'll meet a different character 日 rì, which is narrower than 曰 yuē and means "Sun." For this lesson you are only responsible for learning 曰 yuē.

2. For an English translation of this passage, see Philip J. Ivanhoe and Bryan W. Van Norden, eds., *Readings in Classical Chinese Philosophy*, Second Edition (Indianapolis: Hackett Publishing, 2005), p. 48. In each lesson, I will provide a reference to an English translation of the relevant text, but I have two strong recommendations. First, do not look at any English translations until after you have completed the lesson. Second, it is a good idea to compare multiple translations of a single text and think carefully about the differences among them. Sometimes, differences are because translators make mistakes. However, differences can also be because of choices translators make about how to balance values like readability and fidelity to the original. For more on these issues, see sections 6.4.2–3 and 7.4.2, below.

Sayings") is the collection of sayings and brief dialogues attributed to 孔子 Kǒngzǐ and his disciples. Kǒngzǐ is better known in the West by the Latinization of his name: "Confucius." He lived from 551 to 479 BCE. The *Analects* is divided into twenty "books" (each of which is about as long as a chapter), and the books are subdivided into "chapters" (some of which are as short as this one, and others of which are as long as a few paragraphs). So *Analects* 17.2 is book 17, chapter 2. The traditional view is that the *Analects* was composed after the death of Kǒngzǐ by his disciples, but there is controversy among contemporary scholars about how and when the *Analects* was composed.[3]

1.3.1. Stative Verbs

Look up the meanings of 近 jìn and 遠 yuǎn in the character list if you have not already done so.

Roughly speaking, we can divide Classical Chinese verbs into transitive verbs (which take a direct object) and stative verbs (which do not). Here 近 jìn and 遠 yuǎn are stative verbs. Stative verbs function something like adjectives in English, because they tell you the "state," or characteristics of something.[4] A stative verb, "SV," following a noun, "N," can make a complete sentence.

---

3. Nerd note: To learn more about Confucius, see the TED-Ed video I scripted, "Who Was Confucius?" *TED-Ed*, https://ed.ted.com/lessons/who-was-confucius-bryan-w-van-norden.

4. Nerd note: Pulleyblank subdivides intransitive verbs into stative verbs and "verbs proper." See Pulleyblank, *Outline of Classical Chinese Grammar*, IV.1–8, especially pp. 23–24. Why not just call stative verbs "adjectives"? Well, Pulleyblank does call them that, but many scholars prefer to call them stative verbs for the following reason. A noun followed by a stative verb in Chinese can be a complete sentence. But, in English, you can't just put an adjective after a noun and have a grammatical sentence. If you said, "Ball red," you would sound like the Hulk. In English, to make a complete sentence with an adjective, we use a form of the verb "to be," but in Chinese they use verbs that do the work of "to-be + adjective" in English. (See also the supplemental section "Sino-Tibetan vs. Indo-European" below.)

Pattern:

> N + SV.
> The N is SV.

Examples:

> 子近。
> The Master is near.
>
> 子遠。
> The Master is far away.

1.3.2. Adverb 相 xiāng

Adverbs are words that modify verbs or adjectives. "Quickly," "foolishly," and "carefully" are examples of adverbs in English. In this lesson, 相 xiāng, "to each other," is an adverb. In English, adverbs can go either before or after the verb they modify: "He *cautiously* opened the door" or "He opened the door *cautiously*." But, in general, adverbs in Chinese must *precede* the phrase they modify.

Pattern:

> ADV + V
> to do V in an ADV way
> to V ADV-ly

Example:

> 相近。Xiāng jìn.
> (They) are mutually close.
> (They) are close to each other.

1.3.3. Nominal Sentences

One of the basic constructions in Classical Chinese is the nominal sentence, which involves a noun or a nominal phrase (i.e., a phrase acting as a noun), N1, another noun or nominal phrase, N2, and the grammatical particle 也 yě.

Pattern:

> N1 N2 也。
> N1 is an N2
> As for N1, it is an N2.

So we might say in English

> The king is a thief.

But in Classical Chinese they would say

> King thief 也。

Or, to replace N1 and N2 with nominal phrases, we would say in English

> Whistling through your nose is irritating to your neighbors.

In Classical Chinese they might say

> Whistling through your nose。 Irritating to your neighbors 也。

(Recall that 。 is the traditional multipurpose mark of punctuation.)

If you look at this sentence carefully, you'll notice that it is a bit different from our previous sample. In "King thief 也," both the N1 and the N2 are nouns. But in "Whistling through your nose。 Irritating to your neighbors 也," the N1 and the N2 are actually verbal phrases. (Intuitively, "irritating to your neighbors" does not refer to a *thing*: it describes something that your whistling *does*.) This is quite common in Classical Chinese: the N1 or the N2 (or both) can be verbal phrases that are acting as nouns. So the meaning of our second sample sentence above is really

> Whistling through your nose is a thing that is irritating to your neighbors.

A final point to notice about sentences with a final 也 in which the N2 is verbal is that they often express states that are ongoing (as opposed to states that have been completed) or are universal generalizations (as opposed to statements that are only true at a particular time).[5]

1.3.4. Putting It All Together

So let's apply what we've learned to the first sentence from the reading:

性相近也。 Xìng xiāng jìn yě.

The occurrence of 也 yě at the end of the phrase makes us suspect that we are dealing with a nominal sentence (and we are). So what are the N1 and the N2? As you become more accustomed to reading Classical Chinese, you will start to develop an eye for quickly spotting plausible nominal phrases (although, as in any language, there will be sentences that puzzle you at first glance). When in doubt, start at either the beginning or the end of the sentence and move in the opposite direction, trying various combinations of characters as candidates for N1 and N2, until you see what makes the most sense.

Let's try starting from the beginning of the sentence. Suppose 性 xìng is the N1. That would make 相近 xiāng jìn the N2. So the sentence would be saying

As for 性, they are things that are 相近.

This is, in fact, the correct way to understand the grammar of this sentence. (If you tried 性相 as the N1, you would quickly realize your mistake: 相 is an adverb that has to come before the verb it modifies, so it would be "dangling" without anything to modify if it were part of N1.) You will notice that 相近 is a verbal phrase, of the form ADV + SV. In addition, the 也 here marks a generalization. If you put all this together, you should be able to work out what Kǒngzǐ is saying. (You may be unsure why Kǒngzǐ is saying this, but you should have a hypothesis about the general sense of the sentence.)

Now, go on and do the same thing for the second sentence in this lesson, which has the same grammar. Once you have a hypothesis for what

---

5. Nerd note: To learn more about nominal sentences, see Pulleyblank, *Outline of Classical Chinese Grammar*, III.1, especially p. 16, and XII.2b, p. 118.

the second sentence means, see if you have a better idea why Kǒngzǐ is saying what he is saying, and what contrast he wishes to draw.

1.4. Supplements

1.4.1. Philosophical Issues: Human Nature

Later followers of Kǒngzǐ debated whether human nature is good, bad, morally neutral, has good and bad elements in it, or is good in some and bad in others.[6] Which of these views is Kǒngzǐ supporting in *Analects* 17.2? Which of these views is Kǒngzǐ ruling out in 17.2?

What does Kǒngzǐ mean by "practices" here? He might just mean "human activities" or "what people do." However, *Analects* 1.1 (the opening passage in the book) says "To learn and then have occasion to practice [xí 習] what you have learned—is this not satisfying?"[7] How would you read 17.2 if you were interpreting it in the light of 1.1?

1.4.2. Sino-Tibetan vs. Indo-European

The Indo-European language family is the group to which all the "Western" and most of the South Asian languages belong: Latin and the Romance Languages that developed from it (such as Italian, Spanish, and French), Greek, the Germanic languages (including the German dialects and English), Sanskrit and its descendants such as Hindi. Classical and Modern Chinese are in a different and (in the opinion of most scholars) unrelated language family: the Sino-Tibetan languages. (As I noted in the Introduction, Japanese, Korean, and Vietnamese are neither Indo-European nor Sino-Tibetan languages, even though Chinese characters were adopted in all these cultures.) Unsurprisingly, there are lots of differences between the Indo-European and Sino-Tibetan language families.

---

6. Nerd note: the followers of Kǒngzǐ came to be known as 儒 rú. In English, we translate this "Confucians," but that is misleading because "Confucian" is derived from the name "Confucius," but as you can see 儒 ("Confucians") in Chinese is not cognate with 孔子 ("Confucius").

7. Ivanhoe and Van Norden, *Readings in Classical Chinese Philosophy*, p. 3.

One major difference is that all the Indo-European languages have forms of the verb "to be" (for example εἶναι in Classical Greek, *esse* in Latin, and अस्ति in Sanskrit). This verb expresses existence ("there *are* mice in the basement"), predication ("the mice *are* happy"), identity ("Clark Kent *is* Superman"), and truth ("*Is* not!" "*Is* so!"). There is no one verb or grammatical construction that performs all of these roles in Classical Chinese. For example, as we have seen, 也 yě performs some of the roles of the verb "to be" in English, but it cannot express the fact that something exists (see Lesson 5).

This difference may have led to some of the characteristic differences between Chinese and Western philosophy. Plato is one of the fathers of Western philosophy, and one of his main concerns was the nature of Being. But there is no way to even say "Being" in Classical Chinese. Consequently, certain metaphysical issues became central to Western philosophy in a way that they almost couldn't have in Chinese philosophy.

If you have previously studied any Indo-European languages, you may notice some other things that seem to be "missing" from my vocabulary list for this reading. The nouns have no number. Is it "nature" or "natures"? "Practice" or "practices"? Verbs also lack number and tense: depending on its context, 近 jìn could mean "am close" or "will be close." They have no mood: depending on its context, 近 jìn could be "let them be close" rather than "they are close."

This might seem to imply that Classical Chinese is vague. Classical Chinese can be vague, but so can any other language. Classical Chinese can also have a level of precision limited only by one's own mind. The key phrase in the previous paragraph is "depending on its context." Context disambiguates most expressions to a great extent. By providing context, a careful writer of Classical Chinese can be as precise as he wishes.

Free practice materials—including quizzes and additional readings—are available at www.hackettpublishing.com/chinese-for-everyone-support.

Lesson 2

2.1. Reading: *Analects* 12.11 (Edited)

齊景公問政於孔子。孔子對曰。君君。臣臣。
父父。子子。公曰。君不君。臣不臣。父不父
。子不子。

2.2. Vocabulary

(Twelve new characters, one new meaning)

齊 (齐) Qí n., Qi (name of a state in what is now 山東 Shāndōng Province)

景 jǐng s.v., to be bright, shining; n., Jing (honorific posthumous name)

公 gōng n., duke (highest hereditary title below the king)

問 (问) wèn t.v., to ask someone (indirect object) about something (direct object)

政 zhèng n., government, governing

於 (于) yú prep., from, of (in this passage, marks indirect object of verb)

孔 Kǒng n., Kong (the family name of 孔子 Kǒngzǐ, "Master Kong," better known in the West as "Confucius")

對 (对) duì adv., respondingly, in response

君 jūn n., ruler, lord; s.v., to be a ruler, to be a lord, to act as a ruler (should)

臣 chén n., minister; s.v., to be a minister, to act as a minister (should)

父 fù n., father; s.v., to be a father, to act as a father (should)

子 zǐ n., Master; n. -master (honorific title following a family name); n. son; s.v., to be a son, to act as a son (should)

不 bù (tone changes to bú before a word in fourth tone) adv., not (negates verbs or verbal phrases)

2.3. Grammar Notes

Some Titles, Verbal Sentences and Their Negation, the Preposition 於 yú, the Adverb 對 duì, Nouns as Stative Verbs, and Grammatical Mood

Reading 2 consists of two sentences from *Analects* 12.11.[1] I'll give you the rest of the passage in Lesson 5. Look up the words 君 jūn and 不 bù in the vocabulary list for this reading. Now consider the following sentences:

君君 jūn jūn
君不君 jūn bù jūn

The first occurrence of 君 jūn in each of these sentences is a noun and the second occurrence in each of these sentences is a verb. See whether you can work out the meaning of each sentence above based on this grammar. Now look up the other words in the vocabulary list and see whether you can translate the rest of Reading 2, following the same grammatical patterns when you encounter the words 臣 chén, 父 fù, and 子 zǐ.

In order to understand these sentences, imagine that the Master is recommending how people should act in order to have an ideal community, and the Duke is lamenting how people act in a dysfunctional community.

2.3.1. Some Titles: 公 gōng, 子 zǐ, and 王 wáng

A common way of identifying a hereditary ruler is by providing information in the following order: the state he ruled, his name, and his title ("duke" or "king"). In the case of 齊景公 Qí Jǐng Gōng, 齊 is the name of an ancient state governed by a duke, and 景 jǐng (which can mean "bright, shining") is this duke's 諡 shì, "posthumous title," an honorific name given to him after he died. The fact that this title is used shows that

---

1. For an English translation of the complete passage, see Ivanhoe and Van Norden, *Readings in Classical Chinese Philosophy*, p. 36. Remember that if you really want to learn Classical Chinese you have to struggle through the lesson first before you check a translation.

this passage was recorded after this duke died (in 490 BCE), which helps us to date it.

公 gōng, "duke," is the highest hereditary rank below the 王 wáng, "king." During Kǒngzǐ's lifetime, dukes reigned over the small states into which China was divided. In theory, they were all loyal to the king of the 周 Zhōu dynasty, but, in actuality, each state acted independently. (The king at the time this dialogue took place was 周敬王 Zhōu Jìng Wáng.) This increasingly led to war as the states competed for supremacy. Sometimes the dukes themselves were mere figureheads, and the power in a state was usurped by powerful ministers. This was, in fact, the situation that Duke Jǐng was in when Kǒngzǐ talked with him.

Back in Lesson 1, we learned that 子 can be a noun, referring to a "Master," and in the *Analects* this means Kǒngzǐ (Confucius). This lesson introduces several new meanings for 子 zǐ: as a noun meaning "son," and as the corresponding stative verb, "to be a son" or "to act as a son (should)." (As we will see in Lesson 6, 子 can refer to daughters too, but because traditional China was patriarchal, 子 normally means "son.")

Now is also a good time to make explicit another use that we've hinted at: 子 as an honorific title following a family name. 孔子 Kǒngzǐ is technically a family name followed by a title: "Master Kong." You'll see this pattern a lot in Classical Chinese. In later lessons, we'll encounter 老子 Lǎozǐ ("Master Lao"), 莊子 Zhuāngzǐ ("Master Zhuang"), 孟子 Mèngzǐ ("Master Meng"), and others.

2.3.2. Verbal Sentences

In the previous lesson, we read two nominal sentences. In this lesson, we shall read several verbal sentences. Nominal and verbal sentences are the two basic classes of sentences in Chinese.

At its simplest, a verbal sentence may consist of only one word: a verb. A verb should have a subject, but the subject will often be implicit in Chinese. (In other words, you may be able to guess it from context, so that you don't have to state it explicitly in the sentence.) A transitive verb must have a direct object, and direct objects are *usually* explicit.[2] Some verbs, but not all, also have an indirect object.

In English, "the ball" is the direct object of the transitive verb "hit" in the sentence "He hit the ball." In the sentence "He gave the letter to her," "letter" is the direct object of the verb "gave," and "her" is the indirect object. Sometimes the indirect object is marked with a preposition. In the previous sample sentence, "to" marks "her" as the indirect object. But other times there is no preposition: In "He gave her it," we just know from word order that "her" is the indirect object and "it" is the direct object.

In this lesson, 問 wèn, "to ask," is a transitive verb. In this case, it takes both a direct object (the topic that is asked about), and an indirect object (the person the question is asked of). The other verbs in this lesson are all stative verbs.[3]

2.3.3. The Preposition 於 yú

The English language loves prepositions, and we have a lot of them: "in," "on," "of," "with," "than," and others. Chinese (both Classical and Modern) has fewer prepositions and uses them less often. The most common preposition you will see in Classical Chinese is 於 yú. We see it in this lesson, where it marks the indirect object of the verb 問, the person of whom the question is asked. 於 has lots of other functions, though. It usually occurs in between a verb and a noun.[4]

---

2. Nerd note: Direct objects "disappear" in the presence of certain negative adverbs. See the grammar notes for Reading 4, under "Some Pronouns," for an example.

3. Nerd note: You might think that 曰 yuē is also a transitive verb, but technically it is not. 曰 does not function like a normal transitive verb in that its direct object cannot be replaced by the third-person pronoun 之 zhī, "it." (We shall encounter 之 as a pronoun in Lesson 4.) What follows 曰 is called its "complement," not its direct object.

4. Nerd note: For some examples, see Kroll, *A Student's Dictionary of Classical and Medieval Chinese*, p. 567.

2.3.4. The Adverb 對 duì

Recall that, in Classical Chinese, it is generally true that adverbs precede the word they modify. We saw one adverb in Lesson 1: 相 xiāng, "to each other." Similarly, in this reading, 對 duì, "responding-ly, in response," comes before the word it modifies, 曰 yuē, "to say," describing the manner in which Kǒngzǐ spoke.

2.3.5. Nouns as Stative Verbs

This lesson illustrates a characteristic feature of Classical Chinese: nouns can sometimes act as verbs. When a noun in Chinese is used as a verb, it can be either transitive or stative. In this reading we see nouns acting as stative verbs. The stative verb corresponding to a given noun, N, means "to act as an N."

Pattern:

N → to act as an N[5]

Example:

臣臣 Chén chén

Ministers act as ministers.

So the first 臣 in the example above is a noun, and the second is a stative verb.[6]

2.3.6. Verbal Negation with 不 bù

There are several different words in Classical Chinese that change a verb into a negative. (Words of this kind are called "negative adverbs.") In this

---

5. The symbol → will be used to indicate a grammatical transformation that a word or expression can undergo.

6. Nerd note: As we shall see in Lesson 3 and Lesson 6, if the verb were used transitively, it would mean "to treat as an N" or "to make into an N." So 臣之 chén zhī means "(He) treated him as a minister" or "(he) made him into a minister."

reading we meet the most common of these negative adverbs: bù, "not." Note that 不 can only come in front of a verb or a verbal expression. (We'll learn how to negate nouns and nominal expressions in Lesson 6.)

2.3.7. Implicit Mood

Grammatical "mood" is difficult to define abstractly, but examples of sentences with different moods would be stating something (declarative mood), commanding something (imperative mood), or expressing a wish (optative mood).

Kǒngzǐ's comment raises an interesting translation issue: What mood should it be translated into? Certainly, Kǒngzǐ is not describing how things actually are in his own society. So perhaps we should say that he is expressing a sort of ethical imperative: "Let rulers act as rulers. . . ." But he might be said to be describing what is the case in an ideal society. We might get at this by translating, "True rulers act as rulers. . . ."

2.4. Supplement
2.4.1. Philosophical Issues: Role Ethics

One characteristic of modern ethical thought is that it tends to abstract from a person's ethical roles. This has certain advantages, since it makes us think of humans as possessing intrinsic value or dignity. However, Kǒngzǐ emphasizes following our ethical roles, which has at least two advantages. First, if we think of ourselves as occupying a role, we usually know what our ethical obligations are. It is not too hard to know that, as a student, I should complete my assignments, be prepared for class, etc. Second, as a matter of fact, we do occupy roles, and any ethic that ignores this risks being too abstract.

When she was six years old, my daughter, who reads a bit of Chinese, made an interesting observation about this passage: "He doesn't say anything about mommies and daughters, so they must already have been doing everything okay." Then she said, "Actually, he doesn't talk about lots of people."

In general, how would Kǒngzǐ apply what he says to other groups of people?

Free practice materials—including quizzes and additional readings—are available at www.hackettpublishing.com/chinese-for-everyone-support.

Lesson 3

3.1. Readings: *Analects* 12.22, *Analects* 4.2, and *Analects* 6.23

樊遲問仁。子曰。愛人。問知。子曰。知人。

子曰。仁者安仁。知者利仁。

子曰。知者樂水。仁者樂山。

3.2. Vocabulary

(Twelve new characters)

樊 Fán n., Fan (a family name)

遲 (迟) Chí n., Chi (a personal name)

仁 rén s.v., to be fully human; to be benevolent; n., humaneness; benevolence

愛 (爱) ài t.v., to love

人 rén n., others, other people

知 zhī t.v., to know, to understand, to appreciate; zhì n., wisdom; s.v., to be wise (N.B.: When it is a noun or a stative verb 知 is pronounced zhì, but when it is a transitive verb 知 is pronounced zhī.)

者 zhě g.p. (follows a verbal phrase, transforming it into a nominal phrase describing the subject of the verbal phrase: "those who. . ." or "that which. . .")

安 ān n., peace, safety; t.v., to regard as peaceful

利 lì n., profit, benefit; t.v., to treat as profitable, to treat as beneficial

樂 (乐) lè t.v., to delight in (look under yuè in Kroll, p. 578)

水 shuǐ n., water; n., rivers

山 shān n., mountains

3.3. Grammar Notes

Chinese Names, Transitive Verbs, Reading Pronunciations
讀音 dúyīn, Nouns as Attributive Verbs, Nominalizing with 者 zhě

This reading combines comments on the Confucian virtues of 知 zhì and 仁 rén, taken from three different passages: portions of *Analects* 12.22, *Analects* 4.2, and *Analects* 6.23.[1]

---

1. For English translations, see Ivanhoe and Van Norden, *Readings in Classical Chinese Philosophy*, pp. 37, 10, 19 (respectively).

3.3.1. Chinese Names: 姓 xìng and 名 míng

In the first passage in this lesson, we have the full name of Kǒngzǐ's disciple 樊遲 Fán Chí. In Chinese, a family name is called a 姓 xìng. In English, we often call this a "surname" or "last name," but that is misleading, since in Chinese (and Japanese) the family name comes first when giving someone's full name. In Chinese, one's personal or "given" name is called a 名 míng, and it comes second.[2] Thus, this disciple's 姓 is 樊 and his 名 is 遲.[3] Kǒngzǐ's full name, incidentally, is 孔丘 Kǒng Qiū.

3.3.2. Transitive Verbs

To review: Classical Chinese has both stative verbs and transitive verbs. We saw stative verbs in both Lesson 1 (近, 遠) and Lesson 2 (君 in the sense of "to act as a ruler," etc.). Transitive verbs are verbs that take a direct object. For example, "hit" in English takes a direct object: "hit the ball," "hit the other boxer," etc. Some transitive verbs also can take an indirect object: "give the ball to *her*," "do my chores for *me*," and so on. We met one transitive verb in Lesson 2: 問 wèn, which we saw in the expression 問政於孔子 wèn zhèng yú Kǒngzǐ, where 政 zhèng, "governing," is the direct object, and 於 yú , "of," comes before the indirect object. In the first selection in this lesson we see 問 wèn again, but this time only the direct object is explicit. (The indirect object, whom he is asking the question of,

---

2. Nerd note: In Classical Chinese, both family names and personal names are usually one character long. However, there are exceptions: 公孫 Gōngsūn "Duke grandson" or "Dukeson" is a two-character family name. In Modern Chinese, family names are usually one character long, while personal names are usually two characters long. (Again there are exceptions.) Contemporary Chinese use the family-name personal-name order when speaking Chinese, but when they speak English they may reverse them for the benefit of English speakers. Sometimes you may not be sure which they have done. So if you are unsure what a Chinese person's personal name is, guess that it is the two-syllable part of their name.

3. Nerd note: Technically, this disciple's personal name is 須 Xū, and his "style" (see 4.3.1) was 子遲 Zǐchí, but he was generally known as 樊遲 Fán Chí.

is understood from context.) We also meet two other transitive verbs in this selection: 知 zhī, to know, and 愛 aì, to love.

3.3.3. Reading Pronunciations 讀音 dúyīn

We have seen that many characters can be used in different grammatical classes (as a noun, transitive verb, or intransitive verb). Usually, characters are pronounced the same way in every use. But sometimes a special use of a character has a special reading. For example, 知 is normally a transitive verb ("to know"). In this sense, it is read zhī. But if it is either a noun ("wisdom") or stative verb ("to be wise"), it is read zhì. This is called a 讀音 dúyīn, "reading pronunciation," because such pronunciations are normally only used by scholars when reading Literary Chinese, not in vernacular speaking or reading.

A situation that seems similar but is importantly different is when one character has two distinct pronunciations and meanings in Modern Chinese (and not just when reading Literary Chinese). For example, 樂 is ambiguous in both Literary and Modern Chinese. In this lesson, 樂 is read lè, and means "joy" or "to take joy in." But 樂 can also be read yuè and means "music."[4] One ancient Chinese text makes use of this ambiguity for a visual pun: 樂樂也. Can you see what this means?[5]

3.3.4. Attributive Use of Nouns

We saw in Lesson 2 that a noun like 臣 chén, "minister," can function as a stative verb, "to act as a minister." Nouns can also be used as transitive verbs. When a noun, N, is used transitively like this, it means either "to make it N" (the causative use) or "to treat it as N" (the attributive or

---

4. Nerd note: The two occurrences of 樂 lè in the portion of *Analects* 6.23 in this lesson are sometimes given the 讀音 dúyīn of yào, but this is not a common reading.
5. This was probably a literal pun in the original text. It means "Music is a joy." This comes from the chapter "Explanation of Words and Language" from the *Explanation of Names* (釋名： 釋言語 Shì míng: Shì yányǔ).

denominative use). In the second selection of this lesson, we have two examples of the attributive use of a noun: 利 lì, which is typically a noun meaning "profit" or "benefit," is used attributively to mean "to regard as profitable" or "to regard as beneficial." Similarly, 安 ān is typically a noun meaning "peace, safety," but in this lesson it is used attributively to mean "to regard as peaceful." (In Lesson 6 we'll see a noun used as a verb causatively.)

3.3.5. Nominalizing with 者 zhě

The character 者 zhě is a grammatical particle that takes a verbal expression and transforms it into a nominal expression describing the subject or topic of the verb. Roughly, putting 者 after a verb takes you from the verb to the thing the verb is about.[6]

Pattern:

> V 者 zhě
> that which V's
> that which is V

Examples:

> 仁者 rén zhě
> those who are humane
> those who are benevolent

> 愛者
> those who love

3.4. Supplements

3.4.1. Philosophical Issues: The Virtues of Wisdom and Benevolence

The passages in this lesson discuss two key Ruist (Confucian) virtues: wisdom and benevolence.

---

6. Nerd note: For more see Pulleyblank, VII.2c, and Kroll, p. 597, sense 1.

Some ethical systems emphasize following rules ("Thou shalt not steal. Thou shalt not murder."). Other ethical systems emphasize producing the best consequences ("the greatest happiness for the greatest number of people"). But Confucian philosophers emphasize cultivating virtues and hold that being a good person and acting well go beyond any simple formula that can be put into rules or added up like an accountant's report.

In reading the first passage, your instinct might be to assume that Kǒngzǐ is *defining* benevolence and wisdom. But how would you read it differently if you thought he was simply giving examples of *aspects* of these virtues?

Do *only* the benevolent find benevolence peaceful? Do *only* the wise find it beneficial? Why?

What are some characteristics we associate with water flowing in rivers? What about characteristics of mountains? How might these characteristics appeal to a wise or benevolent person?

In your opinion, is there anything to being a good person other than being benevolent and wise?

3.4.2. Commentaries and Traditional Tones

How are you supposed to know what part of speech 知 represents? In this lesson, we can figure it out from context. However, Chinese commentaries will often help you. For example, one commentary on *Analects* 12.22 says 上知去聲。下如字。[7] This means: "The former 知 is departing tone. The latter [occurrence of the character] is like the character [is normally read]." Okay, so what is a "departing tone"?

Traditional commentaries use the Tang dynasty system of tones, which roughly corresponds to modern tones as follows:

平 píng "level": corresponds to first and second tone in modern Mandarin: mā, má

---

7. This is from Zhū Xī's *Collected Commentaries on the "Four Books"* (discussed in Lesson 9).

上 shàng "rising": corresponds to third tone in modern
Mandarin: mǎ

去 qù "departing": corresponds to fourth tone in modern
Mandarin: mà

入 rù "entering": unfortunately, this could be any of the
four modern Mandarin tones.

If this all seems a little overwhelming (and I cannot blame you if it does),
just remember that if a commentary bothers to tell you something like
上知去聲, it is warning you that a word is doing something you may not
expect it to be doing.[8]

Free practice materials—including quizzes and additional readings—are
available at www.hackettpublishing.com/chinese-for-everyone-support.

---

8. For a more detailed discussion of tones in commentaries, see Paul Rouzer,
A New Practical Primer of Literary Chinese (Harvard East Asian Monographs,
2007), pp. 23–25.

Lesson 4

4.1. Readings: *Analects* 2.17, *Classic of the Way and Virtue* 33

子曰。由。誨汝知之乎。知之為知之。不知為不知。是知也。

知人者知也。自知明也。勝人者有力也。

自勝者強也。

4.2. Vocabulary

(Thirteen new characters)

由 Yóu n., You (personal name [名] of one of Kǒngzǐ's disciples)

誨 huì t.v., to teach someone about something

汝 rǔ n., you (second-person singular pronoun, used to address subordinates)

之 zhī n., him, her, them, it (third-person pronoun; must be the object of a verb or preposition)

乎 hū g.p. (comes at the end of a sentence, transforming it into a question)

為 (为) wéi v., to act as

是 shì n., this

自 zì n., self, oneself (reflexive pronoun)

明 míng s.v., to be enlightened

勝 (胜) shèng t.v., to defeat, to conquer

有 yǒu t.v., to have

力 lì n., strength, power

強 (强) qiáng s.v., to be strong, to be powerful

4.3. Grammar Notes

Styles 字 zì, Pronouns 汝 rǔ, 之 zhī, and 是 shì, Questions with 乎 hū, Equational Verb 為 wéi, Reflexive Pronoun 自 zì

The first passage is the complete text of *Analects* 2.17. The second passage is part of the *Classic of the Way and Virtue* (道德經 Dào dé jīng) chapter 33.[1] (We'll read a longer selection from this work, and talk about its reputed author, 老子 Lǎozǐ in Lesson 6.)

---

1. For English translations, see Edward Slingerland, trans., *Confucius: Analects: With Selections from Traditional Commentaries* (Indianapolis: Hackett Publishing, 2003), p. 13, and Ivanhoe and Van Norden, *Readings in Classical Chinese Philosophy*, p. 179.

Once you have learned the new characters in this lesson, you may be able to figure out the meaning of most of the sentences. Here are a couple of hints to help you out. The character 誨 takes both a direct object (the person whom one teaches) and an indirect object (the thing that one teaches to that person). In this reading, the indirect object of 誨 is 知之. The phrase 知之 could occur by itself as a complete verbal sentence: "(She) knows it." But in the reading it is acting as a nominal phrase ("knowing it").

是知也 is a nominal sentence in which the pronoun 是 refers back to the previous two sentences.

Now, go to the reading and try to understand it (assuming you have already learned the characters), then come back and finish these notes.

4.3.1. More on Names: Styles 字 zì

The first passage in this lesson quotes Kǒngzǐ addressing one of his disciples. Since the disciple is Kǒngzǐ's "subordinate," he addresses him using the disciple's 名 míng, which in this case is 由 Yóu. See the grammar notes for the previous lesson if you've forgotten that term. (Confusingly, this míng is romanized with the same spelling as the English second-person pronoun, as in "Hey, you!" But here "Yóu" is a name, pronounced like the "yo" in "yo-yo.")

What if you didn't have me to tell you that 由 is a name here? Many dictionaries do not list proper names.[2] This is one of the ways in which traditional Chinese commentaries on the classics can be invaluable. They will tell you that

由。孔子弟子。姓仲。字子路。

弟子 dìzǐ n., disciple
字 zì n., style, courtesy name

---

2. Nerd note: For example, Kroll (p. 564) does not tell us that 由 is a proper name, but it does inform us that 由 commonly means "deriving from, out of; by way of, following from," and (more esoterically) that it is part of an expression 由延 yóuyán, which means "the distance an oxcart can travel in a day."

This means "由 is a disciple of Kǒngzǐ. His family name is 仲 Zhòng. His style is 子路 Zǐlù."[3] A "style" or "courtesy name" is a polite name used by others who are not on intimate terms with the person. Kǒngzǐ also has a 字. It is 仲尼 Zhòngní.

There is an interesting use of 字 in chapter 25 of the *Classic of the Way and Virtue*. The text describes the ultimate metaphysical basis of the universe: "There is a thing confused yet perfect, which arose before Heaven and earth. . . . One can regard it as the mother of Heaven and earth."[4] The text then continues:

吾不知其名，字之曰道。

吾 wú n., I (see Lesson 5)
其 qí n., its (see Lesson 6)
道 dào n., Way (see Lesson 6)

Try to translate this phrase, and then check the footnote.[5]

4.3.2. Some Pronouns: 汝 rǔ, 之 zhī, and 是 shì

This reading introduces three common pronouns. 汝 rǔ is a second-person singular pronoun. In other words, it means "you." It is also a term used only to address social subordinates or possibly social equals with whom one is very intimate and casual. So Kǒngzǐ can use this term to

---

3. Nerd note: This is from Zhū Xī, *Collected Commentaries on the "Four Books"* (朱熹，四書集註), which we shall discuss in Lesson 9. The first phrase in the commentary is a compressed way of writing 由。孔子之弟子也。 The 姓 and 字 are transitive verbs: "is-family-named" and "is-styled."
4. Ivanhoe and Van Norden, pp. 174–75.
5. "I do not know its name. Styling it, [I] call [it] 'Way.'" In other words, the author of chapter 25 is saying that there is not a name in Chinese for this "mother of Heaven and earth," but he will use the term "Way" to refer to it. Because the author does not claim intimate familiarity with this entity, he prefers to give it a "style." This passage may record the origin of the use of the term "Way" to refer to a metaphysical entity.

address his disciple, but it would be considered disrespectful for his disciple to use the term to address Kǒngzǐ.

The character 之 zhī is a third-person singular or plural pronoun, but it can only be used when it is the object of a verb or preposition. So zhī can mean "him," "her," or "them," but it cannot mean "he," "she," or "they." It can also mean "it," but only when it is the object of a verb or preposition, and not when it is the subject of a verb. So you can say

汝知之 Rǔ zhī zhī. You know him.

But you cannot say

之知汝 He knows you. ← No! No! No! Bad Chinese
sentence!

Notice also that while we see 之 zhī in

知之 Zhī zhī. (You) know it.

the pronoun disappears when the negative is added:

不知 Bù zhī. (You) do not know (it).

It turns out that 之 generally drop out when 不 bù negates the verb.[6]

是 shì means "this," as opposed to "that" (彼 bǐ). 是 often refers, as it does in the current reading, back to a complex phrase, which is "resumed" by 是, so that it can be commented on by the remainder of the sentence. Imagine a sentence like this: "Blah, blah, blah, blah—*this* (complicated thing I was just talking about) is-such-and-such." That is what is happening in the current reading: two complex phrases are "resumed" by 是 and then commented on.

4.3.3. Forming Questions with 乎 hū

There are ways of forming questions that exist in English but have no analogues in Classical Chinese; there are ways of forming questions that exist

6. Nerd note: Other pronouns in Classical Chinese also do unusual things in the presence of negatives. See Pulleyblank, IX.1e, pp. 84–85 for more on this.

in both languages; and there are ways of forming questions in Classical Chinese that have no analogues in English.

In English, you can make a statement into a question by raising your tone at the end of a sentence. We express this in contemporary writing with a question mark. Compare "You're going to the store" and "You're going to the store?" Perhaps something like this was possible in spoken Chinese in the Classical period, but it is not permissible in the written language.

In both English and Chinese, there are special question-marking pronouns and adverbs, like "who," "what," "where," "when," and "why." In addition, in Chinese (but not English) there are particles found at the ends of sentences that transform a statement into a question. One of the most common of these is 乎 hū.[7]

Pattern:

S → S 乎

It is the case that S. → Is it the case that S?

Example:

汝知之。 → 汝知之乎。

You know it. → Do you know it?

4.3.4. Equational Verb 為 wéi

The character 為 wéi has several uses in Classical Chinese. One of its basic functions is as a verb meaning "to be." In this sense, its use is similar to the 也 yě construction we studied in Lesson 1. However, 為 seems to have connotations of being something for a limited duration, or being

———————

7. Nerd note: 乎 is roughly equivalent to 嗎 ma in contemporary Chinese or か ka in contemporary Japanese.

something only for a special purpose, or of becoming something. Consequently, the construction we see in this reading,

N1 為 N2

(where N1 and N2 are verbal phrases acting as nouns) probably has a sense like

to treat a case of N1 as N2.[8]

4.3.5. Reflexive Pronoun 自 zì

自 zì is a reflexive pronoun. In other words, it is a pronoun that refers back to the subject of the verb, like "himself," "herself," or "itself" in English.[9] It can act as the object of a transitive verb or it can emphasize the agent of the verb. It must come before the verb.[10]

Pattern:

自 TV
(She) TV herself

自 SV
(She) herself SV.

Examples:

自知 Zì zhī
(She) knows herself

自問孔子 Zì wèn Kǒngzǐ
(She) asked Kǒngzǐ herself.
(She) herself asked Kǒngzǐ.

---

8. Nerd note: For more on 為 wéi, see Pulleyblank, III.2, pp. 20–21.
9. Nerd note: Compare 自己 zìjǐ in Modern Chinese.
10. Nerd note: For more, see Pulleyblank, XIII.4a, p. 136.

4.4. Supplements

4.4.1. Modern Chinese Comparison: 是 shì

If you know Modern Chinese, you will recognize the character 是 shì as the "equational verb" in Modern Chinese sentences like 我是美國人 wǒ shì Měiguórén, "I am an American." This use is distinct from the use of the character in Classical Chinese. One difference is that 是 in contemporary Chinese is negated by 不, because it is a verb, but 是 in Classical Chinese cannot be negated by 不 because it is a pronoun, not a verb. So, in case you know Modern Chinese, do NOT translate 是 in Classical Chinese as if it were being used as it is in contemporary Chinese.[11] However, the contemporary usage did evolve out of the Classical use. Consider a sentence of the form "Blah, blah, blah, blah—this (complicated thing I was just talking about) is-such-and-such." If the "blah, blah, blah, blah" and the "is-such-and-such" are both noun phrases, and the "this" is 是, then we have a use that at least looks similar to the modern equational verb use.

4.4.2. Two Phonetic Loans: 女 nǚ and 汝 rǔ

I should confess that I have misrepresented the *Analects* passage in this lesson. The text actually has 女 (which normally is pronounced nǚ and means "woman") rather than 汝 rǔ. However, in the *Analects*, 汝 is always written as 女. (There is only one passage in the *Analects* in which 女 actually means "woman.") So if you were reading *Analects* 2.17 out loud, you would pronounce 女 as rǔ rather than as nǚ. If you didn't already know this, a traditional commentary would tell you that 女音汝, meaning "the character 女 is pronounced as [音 yīn] the character 汝."[12]

So the *Analects* shows us that, at one point, 女, which means "woman," was used as a phonetic loan for the condescending second-person

---

11. Nerd note: In Lesson 11, we'll see an example where translating 是 as if it were the Modern Chinese equational verb (instead of the Classical Chinese pronoun) would lead to a misinterpretation of a famous poem.

12. See, for example, Zhū Xī's *Collected Commentaries on the "Four Books."*

pronoun. Perhaps people started to find it confusing that the common character 女 could mean both "woman" or "you." Consequently, they started to use the less common character, 汝 rǔ, for the pronoun. The character 汝 was originally a semantic-phonetic compound for the name of a river; 女 is its phonetic component, while the semantic component is the "water radical," the three dots on the left-hand side.

Free practice materials—including quizzes and additional readings—are available at www.hackettpublishing.com/chinese-for-everyone-support.

Lesson 5

5.1. Readings: *Analects* 12.11, *Analects* 6.20

齊景公問政於孔子。孔子對曰。君君。臣臣。父父。子子。公曰。善哉。信如君不君。臣不臣。父不父。子不子。雖有粟。吾得而食諸。

子曰。知之者不如好之者。好之者不如樂之者。

5.2. Vocabulary

(Twelve new characters, two new uses)

善 shàn s.v., to be good

哉 zāi g.p. (exclamatory particle; usually found at the end of sentences)

信 xìn adv., truly, genuinely

如 rú conj., if; t.v., to be like

雖 (虽) suī conj., although, even though

有 yǒu t.v., there is, there exists; t.v., to have

粟 sù n., grain

吾 wú n., I; n., my, mine

得而 dé ér exp., to succeed in V-ing

食 shí t.v., to eat

諸 zhū g.p. (equivalent here to 之乎 zhī hū, "... it?")

者 zhě g.p. (transforms verbal phrase, V, into a gerund, V-ing); g.p. (follows a verbal phrase, transforming it into a nominal phrase describing the subject of the verbal phrase: "those who . . ." or "that which . . .")

好 hào t.v., to be fond of[1]

---

1. Nerd note: In addition to its pronunciation of hào, "to be fond of," the character 好 can also be pronounced hǎo (notice the tone difference), in which case it means "to be good, to be pleasing." This distinction is also preserved in Japanese (好き , "to be fond of," and 好い , "to be good").

5.3. Grammar Notes

Exclamatory Particle 哉 zāi, the Adverb 信 xìn, Subordinate
Clauses with 如 rú and 雖 suī, Fusion Word 諸 zhū,
Gerunds with 者 zhě, Transitive Verb 如 rú

The first passage in this reading is the complete text of *Analects* 12.11, which we read part of in Lesson 2. The second passage is the complete text of *Analects* 6.20.[2]

5.3.1. Exclamatory Particle 哉 zāi

In Reading 4, we saw that there are interrogative particles in Classical Chinese: grammatical words that go (usually) at the end of a sentence and change a declarative sentence into a question. In the lesson, we meet 哉 zāi, our first exclamatory particle: a grammatical word that goes (usually) at the end of a sentence and indicates that the sentence is an exclamation (i.e., it is more emphatic than it would be without the exclamatory particle). Usually you translate such a particle simply by putting an exclamation point at the end of the sentence.[3]

5.3.2. The Adverb 信 xìn

So far, we have seen two adverbs, 相 xiāng, "to each other," and 對 duì, "in response," both of which modified verbs. In this lesson we meet another adverb 信 xìn, but this one modifies the entire complex sentence that follows it: "Truly . . ."

5.3.3. Subordinating Expressions 如 rú and 雖 suī

This lesson introduces two common characters that serve to subordinate one sentence to another: 如 rú, which functions like the English "if" (or

---

2. For English translations, see Ivanhoe and Van Norden, *Readings in Classical Chinese Philosophy,* pp. 36, 18 (respectively).

3. Nerd note: For more, see Pulleyblank, XIV.3, pp. 146–47; Kroll, p. 582.

the Modern Chinese 如果 rúguǒ), and 雖 suī, which functions like the English "although" (or the Modern Chinese 雖然 suīrán). (We also see a new use of 者 in the second passage; I'll discuss that below.)

Patterns:

如 S1 S2

If S1 then S2

雖 S1 S2

Although S1, nonetheless S2

Since these words function so much like their English (and Modern Chinese) counterparts, you shouldn't have too much trouble with them.[4] However, they are combined in a complex sentence in this passage, which makes it slightly more challenging. Just take Duke Jing's statement one part at a time and apply the grammatical constructions to it. Since the 如 occurs first, figure out what the S1 is (the "if-clause") and what the S2 is (the "then-clause"). Now look at the 雖: Is it part of the S1 governed by 如, or part of the S2 governed by 如? And what are the S1 and the S2 governed by the 雖 itself?[5]

5.3.4. Fusion Word 諸 zhū

A "fusion word" is a single character that is grammatically equivalent to two other characters. Often (but not always) these are contractions (like

---

4. Nerd note: Both 如 rú and 雖 suī can either precede or follow the noun that is the subject of the S1. You do occasionally encounter the expression 雖然 suīrán in Classical Chinese. However, in Classical Chinese 雖然 has to be read as a complete phrase, "although it is the case that," and not as equivalent to 雖 alone. For more on 如 and 雖, see Pulleyblank, XV.2b.i, pp. 150–51, and XV.3, pp. 156–57, respectively.
5. Nerd note: In logic, mathematics, and linguistics, we say that expression B is "governed by" expression A, or more technically that expression B is "within the scope of" expression A, if A affects the meaning of B. For example, the article title "Rachel Ray takes joy in cooking her family and her dog" is unintentionally funny because the phrase "her family and her dog" appears to be *inside* the scope of "cooking."

"don't" is a contraction of "do not" or 別 bié in modern Chinese is a contraction of 不要 bú yào). For example, 諸 zhū is equivalent grammatically to either 之於 zhī yú or 之乎 zhī hū (depending on the context). You have not encountered a context in which you might use 之於 yet, but in this lesson we see 諸 used as equivalent to 之乎. Try substituting those characters for 諸 and see what meaning you get.

5.3.5. Making Gerunds with 者 zhě

In the previous lesson, we saw that 者 zhě can follow a verbal phrases V, transforming it into a nominal phrase describing the subject of the verb: the one who V. In a few cases, 者 can transform a verbal phrase into a nominal phrase that refers to the action or quality described by the verb. (In English, we do this with gerunds, verbal phrases ending in -ing.)[6]

Pattern:

> V 者
> the state of V-ing
> a case of V-ing

In some cases, it is unclear which function 者 is performing. This is the case in Lesson 5, where the construction is *probably* being used in the gerundive way, but it might conceivably be intended here in the nominalizing way.

Example:

> 知之者 zhī zhī zhě
> understanding it [gerundive use]
> those who understand it [nominalizing use]

In contrast, in Lesson 4, the 者 is probably being used in a nominalizing way, but it might conceivably be used in a gerundive way. (Can you see how you would translate the relevant passage differently depending on which way you take it?)

---

6. Nerd note: For more, see Pulleyblank VII.2c, pp. 66–67.

5.3.6. Transitive Verb 如 rú

In addition to being a conjunction, 如 rú can also be a verb, meaning "to be like." It often (as in the second passage in this lesson) has the specific sense of "to be like in value" or "to be as good as."

5.4. Supplement

5.4.1. Philosophical Issues: Knowing, Liking, and Delighting In

The first passage suggests that there are practical benefits to having people act in accordance with their social roles. Why might Kǒngzǐ believe this is true? Is it in fact true?

What is the "it" referred to in the second passage? Is Kǒngzǐ just talking about knowing how to play chess? Knowing about astronomy? What is the distinction between knowing, being fond of, and delighting in it? Why is each stage better than the last?

One commentary on the second passage suggests: "'Knowing it' means knowing that there is the Way. 'Being fond of it' means being fond of it without being able to achieve it. 'Delighting in it' means delighting in it when you achieve it."[7]

Free practice materials—including quizzes and additional readings—are available at www.hackettpublishing.com/chinese-for-everyone-support.

---

7. This is from Zhū Xī's *Collected Commentaries on the "Four Books,"* discussed in Lesson 9.

Lesson 6

6.1. Readings: *Classic of the Way and Virtue* 1, *Analects* 5.1

道可道也。非恆道也。
名可名也。非恆名也。
無名。萬物之始也。
有名。萬物之母也。

子謂公冶長。可妻也。雖在縲紲之中。非其罪也。以其子妻之。

6.2. Vocabulary

(Twenty-two new characters, two new uses)

道 dào n., a path; n., a way (of living); n., the right way to follow, *the* Way; n., a linguistic account of a way; n., the metaphysical foundation of the universe; t.v., to give a linguistic account of something

可 ke v., can be . . . -ed

非 fēi v., is-not (used to negate nominal sentences)

恆 (恒) héng s.v., to be constant

名 míng n., name; t.v., to give a name to

無 (无) wú t.v., to lack, to not have

萬 (万) wàn n., ten thousand, myriad

物 wù n., thing; n., kind of thing

之 zhī g.p. (subordinates one nominal phrase to another, showing possession or specification); n., him, her, them, it (third-person pronoun; must be the object of a verb or preposition)

始 shǐ n., beginning

母 mǔ n., mother

謂 (谓) wèi t.v., to say something of someone or something

公冶 Gōngyě n., Gongye (a two-syllable family name; literally "Duke's Smelter" or "Dukesmith")

長 Cháng n., Chang (a personal name)

妻 qì t.v., to give a wife to

在 zài t.v., to be in

縲絏 (缧绁) léi xiè n., fetters, ropes for binding prisoners

中 zhōng n., middle, midst

其 qí n., his, her, its, their

罪 zuì n., crime, fault

以 yǐ v., using, taking, by means of

子 zǐ n., daughter; n., Master; n. -master (honorific title following a family name); n. son; s.v., to be a son, to act as a son (should)

6.3. Grammar Notes

Nouns as Causative Verbs, 可 kě before a Verb, Stative Verbs as Adjectives, Nominal Negation, Unmarked Subordination, Subordination with 之 zhī, Coverbal 以 yǐ, Pronoun 其 qí

The first reading in this lesson is chapter 1 from the *Classic of the Way and Virtue* (道德經 Dào dé jīng).[1] This work has traditionally been attributed to 老子 Lǎozǐ, who was supposedly a contemporary of Kǒngzǐ (who lived around 500 BCE). Consequently, the work is sometimes referred to as the *Laozi*. However, many scholars today believe that Lǎozǐ is a mythical figure, and that the *Dào dé jīng* is a compilation of anonymous sayings that gradually accumulated over centuries. For almost two millennia, the standard text of the *Dào dé jīng* was the version that accompanies the commentary by 王弼 Wáng Bì (who died in 249 CE).[2] However, earlier versions of the text were unearthed from tombs in 馬王堆 Mǎwángduī (Hunan Province, in 1973) and 郭店 Guōdiàn (Hubei Province, in 1993). These versions differ from each other, and from the Wáng Bì version, sometimes in important ways. I selected the version of the passage in this lesson from one of the Mǎwángduī texts,

---

1. For an English translation, see Ivanhoe and Van Norden, *Readings in Classical Chinese Philosophy*, p. 163.
2. Nerd note: Wáng Bì wrote one of the two most important commentaries on the *Dào dé jīng* and also wrote a very influential commentary on the *Classic of Changes*. Tragically, he died when he was only twenty-three years old. When I consider how much he achieved in such a brief life span, I am reminded of comedian Tom Lehrer's quip: "When Mozart was my age, he had been dead for three years."

because the grammar in the Mǎwángduī version is clearer than in the Wáng Bì version.[3]

The second reading in this lesson is the complete text of *Analects* 5.1.[4]

6.3.1. Nouns as Causative Verbs

This reading further illustrates the fact that "word classes" in Classical Chinese are fairly flexible. Specifically, in their first and third occurrences in this reading, 道 dào and 名 míng are nouns ("way" and "name," respectively), but in their second occurrences they are verbs ("to give an account of" and "to name").[5] Some words (like the nouns in this reading) *usually* appear as nouns, and are rare as verbs.

In Lesson 2, we saw nouns used as stative verbs. In Lesson 3, we saw that some nouns, N, act as transitive verbs *attributively*, meaning "to treat as N." Here in Lesson 6, we see a noun acting as a transitive verb *causally*, meaning "to make into N."[6]

Pattern:

N → to make into an N

Example:

遠 → 遠之 Yuǎn zhī.

(He) is distant. → (Someone) put him at a distance.

道 → 道之 Dào zhī.

a verbal account → (She) put it into words.

---

3. Nerd note: There were two versions of the *Dào dé jīng* found at Mǎwángduī. In Lesson 6, I use the "A" version, and in Lesson 4, I use the "B" version.

4. For an English translation, see Ivanhoe and Van Norden, *Readings in Classical Chinese Philosophy*, p. 13.

5. Some translations (including the one in *Readings in Classical Chinese Philosophy*) interpret the verbal use of 道 in this line as "to treat as a path; to walk on."

6. Nerd note: For more, see Pulleyblank, IV.3, pp. 25–26.

6.3.2. 可 kě before a Transitive Verb

The character 可 kě has a number of important uses. In Lesson 6, we see that it can precede a transitive verb, TV, and change its meaning into "can be TV-ed."[7]

Pattern:

> TV → 可 TV
>
> TV → can be TV-ed

Example:

> 名 → 可名 kě míng
>
> to name (something) → (something) can be named

6.3.3. Stative Verbs as Adjectives

As I explained in Lesson 1, stative verbs function similarly to adjectives in English, because they tell you the "state" or characteristics of something. In the current lesson, 恒 héng is a stative verb, meaning "is constant." Like an English adjective, a stative verb can come in front of a noun, describing it.[8]

Pattern:

> SV+N
>
> an N that is SV
>
> an SV N

Example:

> 恒道 héng dào
>
> a way that is constant
>
> a constant way

---

7. Nerd note: For more, see Pulleyblank, IV.1, pp. 23–24, and V.4a, especially p. 42; Kroll, p. 239.

8. Nerd note: For more, see Pulleyblank, IV.2, pp. 24–25.

Review: Notice the following contrast

善道 shàn dào a good way
道善。Dào shàn. The way is good.

The former expression is of the form SV+N; it is a nominal phrase, not a complete sentence.[9] The latter expression is of the form N+SV; it is a complete sentence. See the difference?

6.3.4. Negating Nominal Sentences with 非 fēi

We were introduced to nominal sentences in Lesson 1, and we had another example in Reading 4 (是知也). The first and third sentences in Lesson 6 are also affirmative nominal sentences. So we know how to say in Classical Chinese that one thing is another thing. But how do we say that one thing is *not* another thing? The second and fourth sentences in Reading 6 introduce nominal negation.

Pattern:

N1 非 N2 也
N1 is not an N2.

As is the case with the affirmative version of a nominal sentence, N1 and N2 can be nouns, complex noun-phrases, or verbal phrases acting as nouns. In Reading 6, the second sentence is an example of this pattern.

Example:

非恒道也。 Fēi héng dào yě.

What word in this sentence is the N1? Trick question! There is no N1 stated explicitly in the sentence. It turns out that, in a nominal sentence in Chinese, the N1 can be implied by context. This is different from English, in which we must supply at least a pronoun as the subject of a sentence. In the sentence we're looking at, the only plausible subject is the subject of the

---

9. Nerd note: Okay, in the right context, 善道 *could* be a complete sentence, meaning "to regard the way as good" (if the 善 were being used attributively).

previous sentence, which is 道 dào. So the sentence above is really equivalent to

道非恒道也 Dào fēi héng dào yě.

We now know what the N1 is. The N2 then has to be 恆道 héng dào. So the meaning of the sentence as a whole is

道 is not a 恒道.

The grammar of 非恒名也 is parallel to this.

6.3.5. Unmarked Subordination

In both English and Chinese, grammatical subordination of one phrase to another is often marked by a conjunction, like 如 rú, "if," or 雖 suī, "although." However, both languages also have contexts in which subordination is unmarked, usually for rhetorical or poetic purposes. Think of Caesar's famous "I came, I saw, I conquered." What he really means is, "I came, *and then* I saw what was there, *and then* I conquered *it*." More prosaically, in English, "Do the crime, serve the time," means "*if* you do the crime, *then* you will serve the time." Grammarians call this phenomenon parataxis (when the clauses are coordinate) or hypotaxis (when one of the clauses is subordinate to the other).[10]

The first two pairs of clauses from the *Dào dé jīng* illustrate hypotaxis. The first one is equivalent to something like "If 道可道, then 非恆道," or "道可道, but 非恆道." We find a similar construction in *Analects* 8.1:

是可忍也。孰不可忍也。
Shì kě rěn yě. Shú bù kě rěn yě.

忍 rěn s.v., to endure
孰 shú n., what . . . ? (interrogative pronoun)

This can be endured. What cannot be endured?
If this can be endured, *then* what cannot be endured?

---

10. Nerd note: For more on this in Chinese, see Pulleyblank, XV.1–2, pp. 148–49.

6.3.6. Subordination with 之 zhī

We already met one use of 之 zhī, in Lesson 4: as a third-person object pronoun. Here in Lesson 6 we meet another use: 之 as a grammatical particle that subordinates one nominal phrase to another. Specifically, 之 indicates that one thing belongs to another thing (kind of like the way possessives function in English) or specifies characteristics of a thing (kind of like a relative clause in English).[11]

Pattern:

N1 之 N2
the N1's N2
the N2 of N1
the N2 that is N1

Examples

子之知 zǐ zhī zhì
the Master's wisdom

齊之政 qí zhī zhèng
the government of Qi

知人之君 zhī rén zhī jūn
the ruler who understands others

君之知人 jūn zhī zhī rén
the ruler's understanding others
that the ruler understands others

Notice that, as the last two examples illustrate, the N1 and N2 can be verbal phrases acting as nouns.

---

11. Nerd note: This use of the Classical Chinese 之 zhī is equivalent to the Modern Chinese 的 de, or the Modern Japanese の no.

6.3.7. Coverbal 以 yǐ

以 yǐ is one of the most common words in Classical Chinese. 以 is a transitive verb, meaning "to take." However, some verbs also function as coverbs. A coverb indicates the relationship between a noun and a verb, or one verb and another. Most frequently, 以 means "by means of" or "in order to."[12]

Pattern:

> V1 以 V2
> to V1 in order to V2
>
> 以 N V
> V 以 N
> to V with N
> to V by means of N

Example:

> 以其道誨之
> (He) taught him by means of his way.
> (He) taught him his way.

6.3.8. Pronoun 其 qí

其 qí is a possessive pronoun, equivalent to the English "his," "her," "its," or "their." (其 has other uses in Classical Chinese; we'll encounter some in later lessons.) Technically, in a subordinating nominal construction with 之 zhī, it replaces the first noun and the 之.[13]

Pattern:

> N1 之 N2 → 其 N2
>
> The N2 of N1 → its/his/her/their N2

---

12. For more, see Pulleyblank, V.6a.i, especially pp. 47–48; Kroll, pp. 544–45.
13. For more, see Kroll, pp. 353–54; Pulleyblank, IX.1c.iii, p. 80.

Examples:

子之知 zǐ zhī zhì → 其知 qí zhì
the Master's wisdom → his wisdom

齊之政 qí zhī zhèng → 其政 qí zhèng
the government of Qi → its government

君之知人 jūn zhī zhī rén → 其知人 qí zhī rén
the ruler's understanding others → his understanding others

6.4. Supplements

6.4.1. Textual Variants

Compare the following Wáng Bì version of *Dào dé jīng* chapter 1 to the Mǎwángduī version that we read above:

道可道。非常道。
名可名。非常名。
無名。天地之始。
有名。萬物之母。

You will see that we have a few different words in this version:

常 cháng s.v., constant
天地 tiāndì, n. Heaven and Earth; the universe

Three differences are especially noteworthy. First, the Mǎwángduī version uses the expression 萬物 wàn wù twice, whereas the Wáng Bì version uses first the expression 天地 tiāndì and then the expression 萬物.

Second, notice that the Mǎwángduī version uses 恆 where the Wáng Bì version uses 常. Why? There was a "taboo" in China against using characters that occur in the personal name of a reigning emperor. 劉恆 Liú Héng was emperor from 179 BCE to 157 BCE. During his reign, the text was recopied with 常 substituted for 恆,[14] and later copies

---

14. Nerd note: Texts had to be recopied on a regular basis, because the silk and bamboo they were written on decayed rapidly. (The papyrus that was used to

perpetuated these changes. Consequently, we know that Măwángduī version dates from before 179 BCE.[15] Small differences like that are often very informative.

Third, even in this brief passage, we can see that the Măwángduī version uses the grammatical particle 也 much more frequently. It is generally true that the Măwángduī version is less ambiguous and easier to understand because of its greater use of grammatical particles. Recall the line from the *Dào dé jīng* that we saw in Lesson 4. I used the Măwángduī version in that reading. The corresponding Wáng Bì version lacks the 也 at the end of every sentence in that quotation.

6.4.2. Styles of Translation: Boodbergian vs. Drydenian

Professor Peter Boodberg (1903–1972) offered an interesting translation of the Wáng Bì version of the opening of the *Dào dé jīng*:

> Lodehead lodehead-brooking: no forewonted lodehead;
> Namecall namecall-brooking: no forewonted namecall.
>   Having-naught namecalling: Heaven-Earth's fetation,
>   Having-aught namecalling: Myriad Mottlings'
>   mother.[16]

---

record texts in the ancient Mediterranean had the same problem.) You might know that paper was invented in China, but that didn't happen until around 100 CE, in the Eastern Han dynasty, long after the period that Kǒngzǐ and (supposedly) Lǎozǐ lived.

15. Nerd note: How do we know that the change didn't occur the other way? Maybe the text originally had 常 and copyists just substituted the synonymous 恆 in some versions? One reason is the principle known as *lectio difficilior* ("harder reading"): if there are two alternative readings of a text, the one that involves a more obscure word or grammatical construction is more likely to be earlier. Why? A copyist is more likely to substitute a more common word or one he already knows for one in the original text that is uncommon or that he does not recognize than the other way around. And 恆 is less common a word than 常.

16. Nerd note: The original source is "Philological Notes on Chapter One of the *Lao Tzu*," reprinted in Alvin P. Cohen, ed., *Selected Works of Peter A. Boodberg*

This is an interesting effort at stretching English to its breaking point in order to come up with a rendering that matches the connotations of the original Chinese text (as Boodberg understood those) as closely as possible. However, it is unhelpful as an actual translation, because it cannot be understood by anyone lacking an encyclopedic knowledge of both English and Chinese philology. Boodberg's version illustrates one extreme in philosophies of translation.

A paradigmatic example of the other extreme in translation is presented by the poet John Dryden (1631–1700), who defended his loose renderings of Greek and Latin authors by saying:

> . . . I desire the false Criticks would not always think that those thoughts are wholly mine, but that either they are secretly in the Poet, or may be fairly deduc'd from him; or at least, if both those considerations should fail, that my own is of a piece with his, and that *if he were living, and an Englishman, they are such as he wou'd probably have written.*[17]

The problem with Dryden's approach is that Homer (for example) is not a contemporary Englishman, so if your translation of the *Odyssey* sounds like what a poet living in London would write, you have failed to accurately present the original work. To avoid both these extremes, ask yourself the following questions before, during, and after the translation process.

1. Who is my translation *for*? Am I writing for scholars who I can expect to already know a lot of background, or for undergraduates who are wrestling with this text for the first time, or for casual

---

(University of California Press, 1979), p. 480, but you can also find it in a delightful website: Ken Knabb, ed., "Lao Tzu: *Tao Te Ching* (175+ Translations of chapter 1)," *Bureau of Public Secrets* (October 2004), http://www.bopsecrets.org/gateway/passages/tao-te-ching.htm (accessed March 6, 2019).

17. Dryden, Preface to *Sylvae, or the Second Part of Poetical Miscellancies* (1685), from *Bartleby*, https://www.bartleby.com/204/180.html (accessed August 12, 2018). Emphasis mine.

readers who will be flipping through this work for their book group?

2. Will my translation make sense to my target audience? In other words: is my translation actually into English? This might seem like an obvious point, but you would be surprised how often people come up with "translations" that are little different from Boodberg's in readability.

3. Is my translation faithful to the original text? Is the target audience likely to walk away thinking the original text is expressing just what they would say or (equally bad) embodies some cartoon stereotype about "Oriental culture" [sic] that they were predisposed to believe before they read the text?

6.4.3. Alternative Translations of *Classic of the Way and Virtue* 1

Keeping the preceding principles in mind, what are some of the strengths and weaknesses of the following translations of the opening phrases of the Wáng Bì version of the *Dào dé jīng*?[18]

"Tao can be talked about, but not the Eternal Tao. Names can be named, but not the Eternal Name." (John C. H. Wu, *Tao Teh Ching* [New York: St. John's University Press, 1961])

"The TAO, or Principle of Nature, may be discussed [by all]; it is not the popular or common Tao [i.e., the *tao-li* of ethics dealing with the 四端 and the 五常]. Its Name may be named [i.e., the TAO may receive a designation, though of itself it has none]; but it is not an ordinary name, [or name in the usual sense of the word, for it is a presentment or εἰδωλον of the Infinite]." (Frederick Henry Balfour, *Taoist Texts* [London: Trubner & Co., 1884], p. 2; glosses in original)

---

18. I discovered some of these translations via Knabb, "Lao Tzu: *Tao Te Ching*," but have confirmed the translations and publication data.

"The Way that can be told of is not an Unvarying Way;
  The names that can be named are not unvarying names."
(Arthur Waley, *The Way and Its Power* [New York: Grove
Press, 1958], p. 141)

"That Which Is Called The Tao Is Not The Tao

The flow of energy. . . .

Here . . .

It . . .

Is . . . " (Timothy Leary, *Psychedelic Prayers: After the Tao
Te Ching* [Poet's Press, 1966])[19]

Free practice materials—including quizzes and additional readings—are
available at www.hackettpublishing.com/chinese-for-everyone-support.

---

19. Nerd note: Younger readers may not have heard of Timothy Leary. He
became infamous in the 1960s for advocating the alleged philosophical and ther-
apeutic benefits of ingesting large amounts of hallucinogens. It shows.

Lesson 7

7.1. Readings: *Analects* 8.7, *Analects* 4.5

曾子曰。士不可以不弘毅。任重而道遠。仁以為己任。不亦重乎。死而後已。不亦遠乎。

子曰。富與貴。是人之所欲也。不以其道得之。不處也。貧與賤。是人之所惡也。不以其道得之。不去也。

7.2. Vocabulary

(Twenty-two new characters, ten new meanings)

曾 Zēng n., Zeng (the family name of one of Kǒngzǐ's disciples)

士 shì n., aristocrat, scholar, warrior[1]

可以 kěyǐ v., can, may

弘 hóng s.v., to be broad (metaphorically or literally)

毅 yì s.v., to be resolute

任 rèn n., responsibility

重 zhòng s.v., to be heavy

而 ér conj., and (joins verbal phrases)

以為 (以为) yǐwéi exp., to take it as, to regard it as

己 jǐ n., self, oneself (can be used attributively of nouns)

不亦 ⋯⋯ 乎 bú yì . . . hū exp., is it not . . . ?

死 sǐ s.v., to die

而後 érhòu conj., and only then

已 yǐ s.v., to stop (contrast 己 jǐ, oneself, and 已 yǐ, to stop)

富 fù n., wealth

與 (与) yǔ conj., and (joins nouns)

貴 (贵) guì n., esteem

人 rén n. people, persons; n., other people

所 suǒ g.p. (transforms following transitive verb into a nominal phrase describing the object of the verb)

欲 yù t.v., to desire

---

1. Nerd note: Distinguish 士 shì from 土 tǔ, "earth." 士 refers to the class of people at the top of the social hierarchy, but at different periods in history this has different connotations. Sometimes those people are primarily warriors, while other times they are primarily scholars. If it helps, 士 is one of the characters that can be used to mean *samurai* in Japanese (although 侍 shì is also used). 士 is also the name of a piece on the black side in Chinese chess (written 仕 if it is on the red side) that is used to protect the general/king.

其 qí n., the (as in "the Way," "the man"); n., his, her, its, their

得 dé t.v., to get, to obtain; v., to succeed in

處 (处) chǔ t.v., to dwell in, to remain in

貧 (贫) pín n., poverty

賤 (贱) jiàn n., low prestige, low social status

惡 (恶) wù t.v., to dislike, to hate (look under è in Kroll, p. 100)

去 qù t.v., to forsake, to abandon

7.3. Grammar Notes

Coverb 可以 kěyǐ, Conjunctions 而 ér and
與 yǔ, Expression 以為 yǐwéi, Reflexive Pronoun
己 jǐ, Particle 亦 yì, Nominalizing Particle 所 suǒ

The first passage in this lesson is the complete text of *Analects* 8.7.[2] It highlights a characteristic feature of Classical Chinese: the use of double negatives to mean a positive. This passage is a quotation from 曾子 Zēngzǐ. We learn from a commentary that

曾子。孔子弟子。名參。字子輿。

Master Zēng was a disciple of Kǒngzǐ. His personal name was 參 Shēn. His style was 子輿 Zǐyú.[3]

After the death of Kǒngzǐ, Zēngzǐ came to be a Master with disciples of his own, which is why there is a 子 zǐ, meaning "master," after his 姓 xìng.

---

2. For an English translation, see Ivanhoe and Van Norden, *Readings in Classical Chinese Philosophy*, p. 24.
3. Nerd note: This is from Zhū Xī, *Collected Commentaries on the "Four Books"* but *not* from his commentary on *Analects* 8.7. It is from his commentary on 1.4, which is the first passage that refers to Zēngzǐ in the *Analects*. See Lesson 9 for more on Zhū Xī.

The second passage is the first half of *Analects* 4.5.[4] Remember from Lesson 4 that 是 shì means "this" and can be used in a nominal sentence to refer back to a complex expression introduced earlier in the sentence. The second half of 4.5 has puzzled some interpreters, because the seemingly obvious way to take the grammar results in the second half of Kǒngzǐ's comment not making sense. Can you see why? The key to understanding this quotation is correctly answering the following question: In the expression 得之 dé zhī in this lesson, what does the pronoun 之 refer to? Normally it refers back to something earlier in the sentence. Here, I think, it refers to something later in the sentence. See also supplement 7.4.2 at the end of this lesson.

7.3.1. Coverb 可以 kěyǐ

In Lesson 6, we encountered the coverb 可 kě, which comes before a transitive verb, TV, and transforms it into a passive construction: can be TV-ed. Here in Lesson 7, we see the expression 可以 kěyǐ, which comes before either a stative verb, SV, or an active transitive verb, TV:[5]

Pattern:

可以 SV
can SV

可以 TV N
can TV N [where N is the object of the transitive verb]

Examples:

可以死。Kěyǐ sǐ.
(He) can die.

可以去之。Kěyǐ qù zhī.
(She) can abandon it.

---

4. For an English translation, see Ivanhoe and Van Norden, *Readings in Classical Chinese Philosophy,* p. 11.
5. Nerd note: For more see Pulleyblank, V.4a, pp. 42–43.

7.3.2. Conjunctions 而 ér and 與 yǔ

而 ér and 與 yǔ are both conjunctions: they join two grammatical units that are of the same type. However, usually 而 joins two verbal expressions, while 與 joins two nominal expressions.[6] This may be a little confusing, because in English we use the same expression, "and," to join both kinds of clauses: "He *and* I jog *and* lift weights" (the first "and" joins two nouns while the second joins two verbal phrases). But in Chinese these functions are usually kept distinct. The exact connotations of 而 vary a great deal depending on context. Sometimes it functions like the English "but" to mark a contrast; other times it suggests temporal sequence, like "I opened the door *and* left the room" or "I opened the door, *then* left the room."

Pattern:

N1 與 N2

N1 and N2

V1 而 V2

V1 and V2

Examples:

汝與子 rǔ yǔ zǐ

you and the Master

有之而不利 yǒu zhī ér bú lì

(She) has it but does not profit from it.

A related expression is 而後 érhòu, meaning "and only then."

---

6. Nerd note: For more on 而, see Pulleyblank V.5a–b, pp. 44–47, and Kroll, pp. 101–2; for more on 與, see Pulleyblank, VII.1a, p. 61, and V.6a.iii, pp. 50–51. We'll also see another use of 與, as a sentence-final interrogative particle, in Lesson 8.

7.3.3. The Expression 以為 yǐwéi

If you treat 以為 yǐwéi as a two-character expression, its meaning is fairly easy to understand in most contexts:

Pattern:

> N1 以為 N2
> N1 以為 V
> (He) regards N1 as an N2
> (He) regards N1 as V

Examples:

> 安以為利。
> (He) regards peace as profitable.

> 安以為難得。
> (He) regards peace as difficult to obtain.

However, 以為 is actually two separate words: the 以, "to take" (from Lesson 6), and 為, "to act as" (from Lesson 4).[7] This is important because (as we shall see in the next lesson) the two words split up in many cases:

Pattern:

> 以 N1 為 N2
> 以 N 為 V
> (She) regards N1 as an N2.
> (She) regards N as V.

Examples:

> 以安為利。
> (She) regards peace as profitable.

> 以安為難得。
> (She) regards peace as difficult to obtain.

---

7. Nerd note: for more, see Pulleyblank, V.6a.i, p. 49.

Which pattern one uses depends on the style of the writer, as well as upon whether the writer wants to emphasize the first noun: "Peace he regards as profitable" (安以為利) versus "He regards peace as profitable" (以安為利).[8]

7.3.4. The Reflexive Pronoun 己 jǐ

The pronoun 己 jǐ is a reflexive pronoun. It is like the English "self" in that it can be the object of a verb ("I shot myself in the foot"), and it can add emphasis ("He himself said it"). Unlike the English "self," 己 can be possessive, like it is in this lesson, where we might translate it "his own." It differs from 自 zì, another reflexive pronoun, which we saw in Lesson 4, in three ways: (1) 自 can only precede the verb, while 己 can precede or follow the verb; (2) 自 can only refer to the subject of the verb, while 己 can refer to the subject or the object of the verb; and (3) 自 cannot be possessive. Notice the similarities and differences among the examples below.[9]

Patterns:

己 TV   or   TV 己
自 TV
she TV herself

己 V
自 V
he himself V

己 N
one's own N

---

8. Nerd note: The reason the N1 以為 N2 construction is grammatically possible is that 以 can be equivalent to 以之 (which almost never occurs: see Pulleyblank, V.6a.i, p. 48). So semantically N1 以為 N2 is equivalent to N1 以之為 N2, "as for N1, (he) takes it as N2," where the N1 is "preposed" for emphasis, and then "resumed" by the 之.

9. Nerd note: For more, see Pulleyblank, IX.1d, p. 83.

Examples:

己知   or   知己

自知

she knows herself

己問孔子 jǐ wèn Kǒngzǐ

自問孔子 zì wèn Kǒngzǐ

he himself asked Kǒngzǐ

己子 jǐ zǐ

one's own child

one's own Master

As I note in the vocabulary list, distinguish 己 jǐ, "oneself," from 已 yǐ, "to stop." The top of the third stroke of the latter character extends above the bottom of the second stroke. (See also supplement 7.4.1 below.)

7.3.5. The Emphatic Particle 亦 yì and 不亦 . . . . . . 乎 bú yì . . . hū

Broadly speaking, 亦 yì is an emphatic particle emphasizing that something is so of this particular thing. Paradoxically, it can sometimes be translated as "also," other times as "particularly," and still other times as "only." Its sense here in Lesson 7 is related to this emphatic use, but it occurs in a fixed expression.[10]

Pattern:

N 亦 V

N is V also.

N is especially V.

Only N is V.

不亦 . . . . . . 乎

Is (that) not . . .?

---

10. Nerd note: For more, see Pulleyblank, XIV.2b.i, p. 141; Kroll, p. 547.

This last phrase is a rhetorical question assuming an affirmative answer: "Is it not such-and-such?" "Yes! It certainly is such-and-such!"

Examples:

吾亦為之 Wú yì wéi zhī.
I too do it.
I especially do it.
Only I do it.

孔子不亦知乎。Kǒngzǐ bú yì zhì hū
Is not Kǒngzǐ wise?

7.3.6. Converting Verbs into Nominal Expressions with 所 suǒ

One helpful way to think about 所 suǒ is as contrasting with 者 zhě. Recall that 者 *follows* a verbal phrase and transforms it into a nominal phrase that describes the *subject* of the verb. For example, 欲之, "desire it," becomes 欲之者, "those who desire it." The particle 所, in contrast, *precedes* a transitive verbal phrase and transforms it into a nominal phrase that describes the *object* of the verb.[11]

Pattern:

TV N → 所 TV
TV N → that which is TV-ed

Examples:

欲之 → 所欲
(she) desires it → that which is desired

妻汝 → 所妻
he gives a wife to you → whom (he) gave a wife to

---

11. Nerd note: For more, see Pulleyblank, VII.2d, p. 68; Kroll, pp. 437–38.

7.4. Supplements

7.4.1. The Sexagenary Cycle

I noted that you should not confuse 己 and 已. Another character easy to mistake for one of these is 巳 sì. If you look the latter character up in a dictionary, you will be told that it is "6th of the 12 earthly branches, associated with the snake as emblematic animal" (Kroll, p. 429)—which probably doesn't clear things up for you. The character 巳 is part of a counting system that dates back thousands of years, to beyond the boundary of recorded history in China. The "Earthly Branches" are based on the twelve-year orbital cycle of Jupiter and are used in conjunction with the ten "Heavenly Stems" (of which 己 jǐ is one) to produce a sixty-unit cycle for numbering days and years in the traditional calendar in East Asia. Cool, huh?[12]

This system is called the sexagenary cycle (六十干支 liùshí gānzhī). It was already in use on the oracle bone inscriptions, the earliest surviving examples of Chinese writing, which date from the thirteenth century BCE. This cycle was originally used to number days, but since the Han dynasty (202 BCE–220 CE) it has been used to number years. For example, the 1911 revolt that overthrew the last Chinese imperial dynasty, the Qing, is called the "Xinhai Revolution" because it occurred in the 辛亥 xīnhài year (the forty-eighth year) of that cycle. Although East Asian countries now officially follow the Gregorian calendar, the sexagenary cycle still plays a role in fortune telling.[13]

7.4.2. Alternative Translations of *Analects* 4.5

If you really want to understand a passage well, read as many different translations of it as you can and think hard about how the translations differ and

---

12. Nerd note: If you are good at math, you will have noticed that combining ten symbols with twelve symbols gives you one hundred twenty possible combinations, not sixty. However, they only use half of them in the cycle. I have never heard a convincing explanation of why.

13. Nerd note: For more on the sexagenary cycle, see Rouzer, pp. 139–40. For lists, see Appendix 1 and Appendix 2 in Kroll, pp. 639–40.

the thought process each translator followed. As an exercise, think through the following translations of *Analects* 4.5. Does the translation allow you to understand what Kǒngzǐ is saying and why he is saying it? (As an exercise, circle the phrases in each translation that correspond to the pronoun 之 in each of the occurrences of the expression 得之 dé zhī, and then draw an arrow from each circle to the word or phrase that it refers to.)

> "Wealth and honors are what men desire; but if they come undeserved, don't keep them. Poverty and low estate are what men dislike; but if they come undeserved, don't flee them." (James Ware, trans., *Sayings of Confucius* [New American Library, 1955]. Ware's translation doesn't make sense in English: Why on earth would anyone think they should not flee "poverty and low estate" that they do not deserve?)[14]

> The Master said, "Wealth and high station are what men desire but unless I got them in the right way I would not remain in them. Poverty and low station are what men dislike, but even if I did not get them in the right way I would not try to escape from them." (D.C. Lau, trans., *The Analects* [Penguin Books, 1979]. Lau has a footnote to the second sentence that reads, "This sentence is most likely to be corrupt. The negative is probably an interpolation and the sentence should read: 'Poverty and low station are what men dislike, but if I got them in the right way I would not try to escape from them.'")

> The Master said, "Wealth and honor are what people want, but if they are the consequence of deviating from the way, I would have no part in them. Poverty and disgrace are what people deplore, but if they are the consequence of staying on the way, I would not avoid them." (Roger Ames and Henry Rosemont, trans., *The Analects of Confucius* [Ballantine Books, 1999]. Ames and Rosemont apparently follow Lau's emendation but without saying so.)

> The Master said: "Riches and honours—these are what men desire, but if this is not achieved in accordance with the appropriate

---

14. Nerd note: James R. Ware was the first person to receive a PhD in "Chinese studies" from Harvard University (1932), but today he is best known for his translation of *Analects* 2.12: "The gentleman is not a robot." I would give you the original Chinese text of that passage, but it wouldn't help.

principles, one does not cling to them. Poverty and obscurity—these are what men hate, but if this is not achieved in accordance with the appropriate principles, one does not avoid them." (Raymond Dawson, trans., *The Analects* [Oxford University Press, 2008]. Clever! What does the "this" refer to?)

The Master said: "Wealth and rank are what men desire, but unless they be obtained in the right way they may not be possessed. Poverty and obscurity are what men detest; but unless prosperity be brought about in the right way, they are not to be abandoned." (William Soothill, trans., *The Analects* [Oliphant, Anderson, & Ferrier, 1910]. Where is he getting the word "prosperity" from?)

The Master said, "Wealth and social eminence are things that all people desire, and yet unless they are acquired in the proper way I will not abide them. Poverty and disgrace are things that all people hate, and yet unless they are avoided in the proper way I will not despise them." (Edward Slingerland, trans., *Confucius: Analects: With Selections from Traditional Commentaries* [Hackett Publishing, 2003].)

The Master said, "Riches and honours are what men desire. If it cannot be obtained in the proper way, they should not be held. Poverty and meanness are what men dislike. If it cannot be obtained in the proper way, they should not be avoided." (James Legge, trans., *Confucian Analects, Great Learning, and Doctrine of the Mean* [Clarendon Press, 1893]. Ingenious! What does the "it" refer to?)

Wealth and rank are what every man desires; but if they can only be retained to the detriment of the Way he professes, he must relinquish them. Poverty and obscurity are what every man detests; but if they can only be avoided to the detriment of the Way he professes, he must accept them. (Arthur Waley, trans., *The Analects of Confucius* [Macmillan Company, 1938].)

Free practice materials—including quizzes and additional readings—are available at www.hackettpublishing.com/chinese-for-everyone-support.

Lesson 8

8.1. Readings: *Analects* 15.3, *Analects*, 15.24, and *Analects* 4.15

子曰。賜也。汝以予為多學而識之者與。

對曰。然。非與。曰非也。予一以貫之。

子曰。其恕乎。己所不欲，勿施於人。

子貢問曰。有一言而可以終身行之者乎。

子曰。參乎。吾道一以貫之。曾子曰。唯。

子出。門人問曰。何謂也。曾子曰。夫子之道。

忠恕而已矣。

8.2. Vocabulary

(Twenty-three new characters, thirteen new uses)

賜 (賜) Cì n., Ci (孔子弟子。 姓端木。名賜。字
子貢。 Kǒngzǐ dìzǐ. Xìng "Duānmù." Míng "Cì." Zì
"Zǐgòng.")

也 yě g.p. (vocative particle; follows name of person
addressed); g.p. (comes at end of sentences to mark
nominal sentences; often indicates a generalization)

予 yú n., I

多 duō adv., to do V of many things

學 (学) xué s.v., to study, to learn

識 (识) zhì t.v., to remember

與 (与) yú g.p. (sentence-final interrogative); yǔ conj., and
(joins nouns)

然 rán s.v., to be so, to be this way

非 fēi s.v., to be wrong, to be mistaken; v., is-not (used to
negate nominal sentences)

一 yi (pronounced yī alone, changes to yí in front of a
syllable in fourth tone, changes to yì in front of any
other tone) n., one

貫 guàn t.v., to bind together

子貢 Zǐgòng n., Zigong (see above under 賜 Cì)

問 (问) wèn adv., questioningly, as a question; t.v., to ask
someone (indirect object) about something (direct
object)

言 yán n., words, maxim

終身 zhōngshēn exp., to the end of one's life (literally, "end
self")

行 xíng t.v., to put into effect

其 ……乎 qí . . . hū exp., Is it not . . .? (expects answer "It
is . . . !")

恕 shù n., reciprocity, sympathy

勿 wù adv., do not . . . it (imperative mood)

施 shī t.v., to bestow something on someone (usually done by a superior to a subordinate)

參 (参) Shēn n., Shen (曾子。孔子弟子。名參。字子輿。 Zēngzǐ. Kǒngzǐ dìzǐ. Míng "Shēn." Zì "Zǐyú.")

乎 hū g.p. (vocative particle; follows name of person addressed); g.p. (marks a question)

唯 wéi v., is-so, yes (suggests prompt and unhesitating agreement)

出 chū s.v., to go out, to leave

門人 (门人) ménrén n., disciples (literally, "gate people")

何 hé n., what (interrogative pronoun)

夫子 Fūzǐ n., the Master

忠 zhōng n., loyalty; dutifulness

而已矣 éryǐyǐ exp., and that is all

8.3. Grammar Notes

Vocative Particles 也 yě and 乎 hū, Sentence-Final Interrogative 與 yú, Stative Verb 非 fēi, Preposing an Object with 以 yǐ, Modal 其 qí and 其 ⋯⋯ 乎 qí . . . hū, Negative Imperative 勿 wù, Interrogative Pronoun 何 hé, Modal Particle 矣 yǐ and the Expression 而已矣 ér yǐ yǐ

You now know enough Classical Chinese to read some more challenging passages. This reading consists of three passages: *Analects* 15.3, *Analects* 15.24, and *Analects* 4.15.[1] These three passages are often interpreted in the light of each other as explaining the central teaching of Kǒngzǐ. They also present some subtleties of grammar.

---

1. For an English translation, see Ivanhoe and Van Norden, *Readings in Classical Chinese Philosophy,* pp. 44, 45–46, 12 (respectively).

8.3.1. Two Vocative Particles: 也 yě and 乎 hū

In this lesson we see unusual uses of 也 yě and 乎 hū as vocative particles. In other words, they follow a name, indicating that the sentence addresses that person. This is related to the use of 也 as a topic marker, which we shall see in a later lesson.[2]

8.3.2. Sentence-Final Interrogative 與 yú

Back in Lesson 4, we learned about the interrogative (question-making) particle 乎 hū. In this lesson, we find the interrogative particle 與 yú. Here it is written with the same character as the noun-conjunction 與 yǔ (but note that it is pronounced with a different tone); however, in some texts the same interrogative particle is written 歟. 與 / 歟 does not function exactly the same as 乎, though. The former is actually a contraction of 也乎 yě hū. Try replacing 與 with 也乎 in the reading.[3]

8.3.3. Stative Verb 非 fēi

We know (from Lesson 6) that 非 fēi is used to form the negation of nominal sentences. It also is a verb meaning "is wrong," which is how it is being used in *Analects* 15.3.[4]

8.3.4. Preposing an Object with 以 yǐ

You might initially be puzzled by the phrase 一以貫之 yì yǐ guàn zhī. It is equivalent to 以一貫之, but with the 一 put out front to emphasize it.

---

2. Nerd note: For more on the use of 也 as a topic-marker in the *Analects*, see Pulleyblank, VIII.5a, pp. 73–74; Kroll, p. 538, sense 2.

3. Nerd note: For more, see Pulleyblank, III.1a, pp. 16–17; Kroll, p. 571.

4. Nerd note: For more on this use of 非, see Pulleyblank, XI.1d, p. 106. If 非 is being used as a stative verb here, why is it followed by 也? Well, 非 is normally used in the pattern N1 非 N2 也, which means "N1 is not N2." From this, 非也 developed as a contraction of N1 非 N2 也.

Written in the normal way, you should find it fairly easy to understand (as long as you know the meaning of the individual characters).

But why is the phrase written the way that it is, and how does it work grammatically? This is actually a little complicated, but you can learn a lot by following the explanation. One way of emphasizing a noun in Classical Chinese is to "prepose" it at the beginning of the phrase, and then "resume" it with a pronoun later. In the English sentence "My favorite book—and he sold it for two dollars!" the nominal phrase "my favorite book" is preposed and resumed by the pronoun "it."[5] In *Analects* 15.3, Kǒngzǐ is essentially saying 以一貫之, but he wanted to emphasize the word 一, so he preposed it. Since that word was preposed, there should be a pronoun following the 以, resuming it. So we would expect to see 一以之貫之. Why don't we? It turns out we almost never see the phrase 以之 yǐ zhī in Classical Chinese, because the verb 以 usually "absorbs" a 之 that would follow it. This is what is happening in 15.3. So we can think of the following grammatical transformations as occurring:

$$以一貫之 → 一以之貫之 → 一以貫之$$

You may still be wondering what the final 之 refers to. In 15.3, it refers to the things that Kǒngzǐ 學而識 (in Kǒngzǐ's initial question): "By means of one thing I bind them [what I study and remember]." The same construction occurs again in 4.15 (the last passage in this lesson), but in the phrase 吾道一以貫之. Here we have a double preposing. 吾道 is a preposed noun phrase resumed by the final 之, and 一 is, as before, preposed before the 以: "My Way—by means of one thing I bind it."

8.3.5. Modal 其 qí and 其 ⋯⋯ 乎 qí . . . hū

In Lesson 6, we saw that 其 qí can be a possessive pronoun, roughly equivalent to "his," "her," "its," or "their." In Lesson 7, we saw that it also has a (rare) use that is roughly equivalent to the definite article "the" in

---

5. Nerd note: For more on preposing a term for emphasis, see Pulleyblank, VIII.1, pp. 69–71 (where he calls it "exposure").

English. Here in Lesson 8, we see the modal use of 其. By itself, modal 其 intensifies an affirmation: "It is really the case that. . . ." In this lesson, the modal use occurs in a fixed expression that indicates a rhetorical question expecting an affirmative answer.[6] Notice that, although 其 ⋯⋯ 乎 is an affirmative in grammatical form, it generally has to be translated into a phrase with a negative in English (simply because we don't use an affirmative form of this rhetorical question in English).

8.3.6. Negative Imperative 勿 wù

Often (but not invariably) 勿 wù acts like a negative imperative that has absorbed the object of the following verb, so that it means "Do not . . . it."[7]
Pattern:

TV+N → 勿 TV

Example:

食之。 → 勿食。
(He) ate it. → Do not eat it.

In *Analects* 15.24 (the second passage in this lesson), we have 勿施於人. Write out what this phrase would transform into if there were no 勿, then read the following footnote.[8]

8.3.7. Interrogative Pronoun 何 hé

We have seen how to form questions using sentence-final interrogative particles (乎 hū and 與 yú). We can also form them by using an

---

6. Nerd note: For more, see Pulleyblank, XII.4a, pp. 123–24.
7. Nerd note: For more, see Kroll, p. 482. There is a series of paired negatives in Chinese, in which the first member of each pair does not absorb the object of a following verb or may indicate an ongoing state, while the second member of the pair absorbs a following verb-object or indicates a perfective aspect: 不 bù/弗 fú, 毋 (無)/wú 勿 wù. See Pulleyblank, XI.1–2, pp. 103–11.
8. Answer: Without the 勿, the phrase would become 施之於人. In the context of 15.24, what does the 之 refer back to?

interrogative pronoun such as 何 hé, "what." Sometimes 何 will be used in one sentence with 乎 or 與, and other times (as in this lesson) it will occur by itself.

8.3.8. Modal Particle 矣 yǐ and Expression 而已矣 ér yǐ yǐ

The sentence-final phrase 而已矣 ér yǐ yǐ can be treated as an idiom, meaning "and this is all." However, analyzing the meaning of this expression gives us a good excuse to learn about the common modal particle 矣 yǐ.

The nuances of the meanings of 矣 yǐ are complex, but as a first approximation, we can say that 矣 is perfective. In other words, 矣 indicates that the action or state described by the verbal phrase is complete, either in time or in degree.[9] If the completion is temporal, it is often best translated by putting the verb in the past or perfect tense (V-ed, have V-ed), and/or by using the word "already." If the quality described by the verbal phrase is complete in degree, it is often best translated by using italics or by using words like "truly," "really," etc.

Pattern:

V 矣

has already V-ed [action has been completed in time]

is really V [quality is complete in degree]

is V

Examples:

子死矣。 Zǐ sǐ yǐ.
The Master has died.

子仁矣。 Zǐ rén yǐ.
The Master is genuinely benevolent.
The Master *is* benevolent.

---

9. Nerd note: For more, see Kroll, p. 546. 矣 yǐ roughly corresponds to 了 le in Modern Chinese. For more on 矣 and the nuances of the 矣/了 comparison, see Pulleyblank, XII.2a, pp. 116–18.

Now, in the expression 而已矣 éryǐyǐ, we know that 而 means "and," 已 "to stop" (again, don't confuse this character with 己 jǐ, *oneself*), and 矣 indicates completion of the action described by the verb. So the expression literally means "and stop completely."

8.4. Supplements

8.4.1. Philosophy: The One Thread

There are a lot of interesting interpretive puzzles raised by these passages. What is the "one thing" referred to in *Analects* 15.3? If all we had were 15.3 and 15.24, we might conclude that the Master's studies are bound together by the ethical goal of achieving reciprocity. In other words, the Master's extensive study of poetry, history, and ritual is not to achieve purely theoretical understanding, but is rather to internalize the moral lessons that they offer, which can be summarized in the adage: do not inflict upon others that which you yourself do not desire. However, in *Analects* 4.15, Zēngzǐ explains to the other disciples that the "one thing" is "loyalty and reciprocity." Wait, aren't those *two* things? And how can loyalty and reciprocity jointly encompass everything that the Master teaches? Perhaps loyalty is not just loyalty to a person but loyalty to the Way itself. But then what does reciprocity add? And would Kǒngzǐ really endorse Zēngzǐ's explanation? After all, he didn't stay around to hear the answer, but left the room right after Zēngzǐ excitedly shouted, "Yes!"[10]

8.4.2. Commentaries: Using 反切 fǎnqiè

The personal name of Zēngzǐ is 參. The entry for this character in Kroll (pp. 31–32) gives the primary pronunciation as cān (meaning "participate in, take part"). But if you really want to impress people, use the

---

10. Nerd note: For an overview of various interpretations of this famous passage (and why I think they are all wrong), see Bryan W. Van Norden, "Unweaving the 'One Thread' of *Analects* 4.15," in Van Norden, ed., *Confucius and the "Analects": New Essays* (New York: Oxford University Press, 2001), 216–36.

讀音 dúyīn ("Reading Pronunciation") and pronounce 參 as Shēn. How do you know that 參 has a special reading here? Yes, read a commentary.

Since Chinese does not have an indigenous alphabet, traditional commentaries came up with a clever technique for representing pronunciations. The 反切 fǎnqiè system represents the pronunciation of a character by providing two other characters: one with the same first consonant as the character being explained and the other with the same final sound as the character being explained. One commentary tells us that

參。所金反。

This means "參 is pronounced with the initial consonant of 所 and the final sound of 金." 反 fǎn marks the preceding words as a 反切 fǎnqiè pronunciation. Now, the way characters were pronounced when the commentary was written is different from the way they are pronounced today. This is great news if your career is about reconstructing how Chinese sounded in the Tang dynasty.[11] But it is bad news if you want to use the 反切 to know how the characters are pronounced now. Nonetheless, 反切 are useful as a heads up that something special is going on with a particular character. (Compare what I said about traditional tones in Lesson 4.)

So, in the present case, when you see that the commentary bothers to give you a 反切 for 參, you know it has a special pronunciation. So you look up 參 under cān in Kroll, and you see that it has a secondary pronunciation of shēn, which refers to the constellation Orion, or to the herb ginseng (人參 rénshēn), and you know that must be its pronunciation in this passage.[12]

---

11. Nerd note: Yes, there are people whose job is to reconstruct the medieval and ancient pronunciations of Chinese. If you think that is silly, remind yourself that there is an entire television channel devoted to nothing but golf. Glass houses, people.

12. Nerd note: Let's convince ourselves that the 反切 system actually works. Zhū Xī's *Collected Commentaries on the "Four Books"* says: 參。所金反。Kroll gives you the Modern Mandarin pronunciation first but then gives you the

8.4.3. A Grammatical Anomaly in 15.24?

This passage actually contains what seems to be a grammatical error. However, the passage reads smoothly, so it succeeds stylistically even if it is in error formally. To see the grammatical error, try to answer the two following questions consistently: (1) What are the verbal phrases that are joined by the 而? (2) What verbal expression is nominalized by the 者 near the end of the sentence? There is no way to consistently answer these two questions.

The conjunction 而 must join two verbal phrases, V1 and V2. The V1 must be 有一言 and the V2 must be 可以終身行之. So far so good. But now what verbal phrase does the 者 nominalize? If it nominalizes the immediately preceding verbal phrase 可以終身行之, then the 而 is joining a verbal phrase to a nominal phrase, which is ungrammatical. If the 者 nominalizes both preceding verbal phrases, V1 而 V2, then all we have is a nominalized verbal phrase instead of a complete sentence. Nonetheless, I think the sentence sounds fine in Classical Chinese. The grammar of the whole sentence is 有 V 者乎: "Is there a thing that is V?" The V is a complex verbal phrase, the most basic form of which is 有言 而行之: "There is a saying and one puts it into effect." When you put this all together, the 有 gets away with double duty, as the main verb of the sentence AND as part of a subordinate verbal phrase (V1 而 V2).

Free practice materials—including quizzes and additional readings—are available at www.hackettpublishing.com/chinese-for-everyone-support.

---

pronunciation in Medieval Chinese ("MC"). From this, we can see that 所 was pronounced *srjoX* and 金 was pronounced *kim*, so the commentary is telling us that 參 is pronounced like *sr* + *im* = *srim*. And the MC pronunciation of 參 corresponding to the Modern Mandarin shēn, "ginseng," is *srim*. Viola!

Lesson 9

9.1. Readings: *Analects* 5.13 and the Commentary by Zhū Xī

子貢曰。夫子之文章。可得而聞也。夫子之言性與天道。不可得而聞也。文章。德之見乎外者。威儀文辭皆是也。性者人所受之天理。天道者天理自然之本體。其實一理也。言夫子之文章。日見乎外。固學者所共聞。至於性與天道則夫子罕言之而學者有不得聞者。

9.2. Vocabulary

(Twenty-four new characters, four new uses)

文章 wénzhāng (see the Chinese commentary within the reading for this lesson)

聞 (闻) wén t.v., to hear

言 yán n., words, maxim; t.v., to put into words, to create maxims; t.v., to mean

天 tiān n., Heaven (an impersonal higher power); s.v., to be of Heaven, Heavenly

德 dé n., virtue, political charisma generated by a good character[1]

見 (见) xiàn s.v., to be visible (look under jiàn in Kroll, p. 199)

乎 hū prep., on, from, of; g.p. (comes at the end of a sentence, transforming it into a question; roughly like 嗎 ma in Modern Chinese); g.p. (vocative particle; follows name of person addressed)

外 wài n., the outside

威儀 (威仪) wēiyí n., august bearing

文辭 wéncí n., eloquent words

皆 jiē adv., all

者 zhě g.p. (marks expression being defined or characterized); g.p. (follows a verbal phrase, transforming it into a nominal phrase describing the subject of the verbal phrase: "those who . . ." or "that which . . ."); g.p. (transforms verbal phrase, V, into a gerund, V-ing)

受 shòu t.v., to receive

---

1. Nerd note: For the meaning and historical development of the concept of 德 dé, "virtue," see David S. Nivison, *The Ways of Confucianism* (LaSalle, IL: Open Court, 1996), especially pp. 15–58.

理 lǐ n., Pattern, Principle (technical term in Confucian metaphysics for the underlying structure of the universe, fully complete in each thing that exists, but manifested differently due to the concrete embodiment of each thing)

自然 zìrán s.v., to be natural (literally, "self-so"); n., naturalness

本 běn n., root, basis; s.v., to be fundamental

體 (体) tǐ n., Substance (technical term in Confucian metaphysics; roughly, the 體 is what something is in itself, while its 用 yòng, Function, is how it manifests itself in action; the eye is 體, seeing is its 用; water is 體, waves are its 用)

實 (实) shí n., reality (as opposed to appearance or manifestation)

日 rì adv., daily[2]

固 gù adv., definitely

共 gòng adv., jointly, as a group

至於 (至于) zhìyú exp., When it comes to . . .

則 (则) zé g.p. (contrastive topic marker)

罕 hǎn adv., seldom

9.3. Grammar Notes

Nouns as Adjectives, Topic Marker 者 zhě, Dropping of Final 也 yě, Contrastive Topic Marker 則 zé, the Expression 學者有 xuézhě yǒu . . ., 得 dé + Verb Construction

This lesson is the text of *Analects* 5.13 and the commentary on that passage by 朱熹 Zhū Xī (1130–1200 CE).[3] The format you see in this lesson,

---

2. Nerd note: Remember way back in Lesson 1 when I told you that we would learn a character, 日 rì, that looks superficially like 曰 yuē, and you should learn to distinguish them?

3. For an English translation of *Analects* 5.13, see Ivanhoe and Van Norden, *Readings in Classical Chinese Philosophy*, p. 15. There is no complete English

classic text in large characters and commentary in small characters, is traditional. Recall that "Classical Chinese" refers to the dialect (really a group of dialects) of written Chinese from around the time of Kǒngzǐ (Confucius) up to the end of the Han dynasty (220 CE), while "Literary Chinese" refers to all the styles of written Chinese up to the beginning of the widespread use of vernacular Chinese in the twentieth century. So the *Analects* is written in Classical Chinese, while Zhū Xǐ's commentary is written in a later form of Literary Chinese.

The grammar and vocabulary of *Analects* 5.13 and Zhū Xǐ's commentary on it are not especially difficult. However, there are many challenging concepts and issues involved.[4] In particular, you need to learn a little bit about Confucian metaphysics.[5] For Confucians, everything in the universe has two aspects: Pattern (理 lǐ) and 氣 qì. Pattern is the structure of the universe. It is fully present and identical in each and every thing that exists. Because we all share the same Pattern, we are part of a potentially harmonious whole that comprises other humans, animals, plants, and the rest of the natural world. One who fully understands the Pattern will be spontaneously compassionate and righteous.

Although the underlying Pattern is the same in everything, it manifests itself differently because each thing has a distinct endowment of 氣 qì. Unfortunately, there is no good English equivalent for 氣. People have proposed "ether," "material force," "psychophysical stuff," and "vital

---

translation of Zhū Xǐ's commentary, but for the complete Chinese text see https://ctext.org/si-shu-zhang-ju-ji-zhu.

4. Nerd note: For an accessible yet scholarly introduction to the issues, read Philip J. Ivanhoe, "Whose Confucius? Which *Analects*?" in Van Norden, *Confucius and the "Analects,"* pp. 119–33.

5. Nerd note: Metaphysics is the branch of philosophy that addresses the questions: What are the most fundamental kinds of things that exist? How are those things related to one another? The "Confucian metaphysics" I describe here is really the metaphysics of the "Neo-Confucians" and not necessarily the metaphysics that Kǒngzǐ himself would have assumed. See supplement 9.4.2 to this lesson.

fluid," among others, but none of those is really a translation because those phrases don't mean anything in English. Basically, 氣 is like a fluid that can condense to form concrete things. How "turbid" or "clear" the 氣 is determines the way in which the Pattern manifests itself. (Imagine the different ways in which sunlight filters through water that is clear, or a little hazy, or almost mud.) (See also Kroll, p. 358.)

9.3.1. Nouns as Adjectives

A further illustration of the flexibility of grammatical classes in Classical Chinese is that one noun can sometimes precede another noun and act as an adjective. We can think of this construction as being elliptical for (short for) the subordinating construction using 之:

Pattern:

> N1 之 N2 → N1 N2
> The N2 of N1

Example:

> 人之性 → 人性
> human nature

9.3.2. 者 zhě as Topic Marker

We have seen 者 zhě used (1) to change a verbal phrase into a description of the subject of that phase (that which V's) or (2) into a gerund (V-ing), which refers to the activity described by the verb. A third use of 者 is simply (3) to emphasize the topic of a sentence.[6] A common instance of this use is to mark a word or phrase that is being defined or characterized. Zhū Xī often uses the word 者 like this to mark expressions from the classical text that he is explaining in his commentary.

---

6. For more, see Pulleyblank, VIII.5c, p. 74.

In its first occurrence in this lesson, 者 is being used in the first way (*that which is* 見於外 xiàn yú wài). In its next two occurrences, 者 is being used in the third way, marking the expression Zhū Xī is defining.

Pattern:

N1 者 N2 也。
N1 is N2
The expression "N1" means N2.

Example:

仁者愛人也。
Benevolence is loving others.
"Benevolence" means loving others.

9.3.3. Dropping Final 也 yě

We see several examples in Zhū Xī's commentary of the fact that the 也 yě can drop out of an N1 N2 也 construction. In some dialects of Classical or Literary Chinese this is quite rare (e.g., in the *Analects*), while in others it is more common (e.g., in the Wáng Bì version of the *Classic of the Way and Virtue*). The style of Zhū Xī's commentary is very concise, so he tends to drop the 也 when he feels that the syntax of the sentence is clear without it.

9.3.4. 則 zé as Contrastive Topic Marker

As a conjunction, 則 zé can mark the then-clause of an "if . . . then . . ." sentence. (It is sometimes found in combination with 如 rú, which we saw in Lesson 5: 如 ······ 則 ······, "if . . . then . . .") Here in Lesson 9, though, 則 marks a topic that is being commented on by the rest of the sentences. When used like this, 則 suggests that the topic is being contrasted with something else.[7]

_____

7. Nerd note: 則 was probably originally a demonstrative pronoun, "this," which had a resumptive use, like 是 often does. Can you see how both its use as a

Pattern:

N1 則 S

As for N1 [as opposed to N2], S.

Example:

性則善。習不然。

His *nature* is good, but his practices are not so.

As for his nature, *that* is good, but his practices are not.

9.3.5. The Expression 學者有······ xuézhě yǒu ...

This phrase is easy to misinterpret. 學者 xuézhě, "those who study," is the *topic* of the sentence: it is *not* the *subject* of the following verb, 有 yǒu. The rest of the sentence is a *comment* on this topic. The verb here means "there are." So, in effect, the initial 學者 tells you *where* or *among whom* there are the things described in the rest of the sentence.[8]

9.3.6. 得 dé + Verb

You can probably guess this one, but just in case you can't: 得 dé + V is the same as 得而 + V, which we encountered way back in Lesson 5 ("to succeed in V-ing")

9.4. Supplements

9.4.1. The Expression 罕言 hǎn yán

There is nothing grammatically challenging about the ADV+V expression 罕言 hǎn yán, "seldom spoke of," in Zhū Xī's commentary. However, Zhū Xī's original audience would have immediately recognized this as a

---

contrastive topic marker and as a conjunction derived from this pronominal use? For more on 則 as a conjunction, see Pulleyblank, XV.2.c.i, pp. 154–55; for more on 則 as a contrastive topic marker, see Pulleyblank, VIII.3, pp. 72–73. See also Kroll, pp. 585–86.

8. For more, see Pulleyblank, IV.7, pp. 30–31.

phrase from *Analects* 9.1: "The Master seldom spoke of profit and fate and humaneness" (子罕言利與命與仁 Zǐ hǎn yán lì yǔ mìng yǔ rén).[9] Zhū Xī is implicitly suggesting that 9.1 is evidence that there were some topics of which the Master "seldom spoke." In other words, Zhū Xī thinks that Kǒngzǐ had esoteric teachings that he only revealed to his most advanced disciples.[10] (Notice how Zhū Xī presents a textual argument in a subtle way by just quoting a text in passing.) So Zhū Xī understands Zǐgòng's comments here in 5.13 as an exclamation of joy when the Master has finally begun to teach Zǐgòng his esoteric teachings about human nature and the Way of Heaven.

9.4.2. Zhū Xī and "Neo-Confucianism"

Zhū Xī is perhaps the third most influential Confucian philosopher (after Kǒngzǐ himself and 孟子 Mèngzǐ, whom we'll read in Lesson 12). Part of the reason for his immense importance is that he devised a new Confucian educational curriculum grouped around the *Four Books: Great Learning, Analects, Mengzi,* and *Mean.* In addition, he wrote *Collected Commentaries on the "Four Books,"* which is the source of the commentary in today's lesson. In 1313, the *Four Books* along with Zhū Xī's commentaries on them became the basis of the civil service examinations, which were one of the primary routes to power, prestige, and pelf in imperial China. Consequently, generations of scholars had to literally memorize all of the *Four Books* and Zhū Xī's commentary on them. Although the examinations

---

9. Dawson, *The Analects,* p. 31.

10. Nerd note: Some religions, sects, and arguably even some philosophers have esoteric teachings that are different from their exoteric teachings. Exoteric teachings are what you tell the public and also beginners among your disciples. Esoteric teachings are doctrines that are hidden from most people and only revealed to advanced students or initiates. Typically, teachings are treated as esoteric because they are so subtle or so shocking that one cannot understand them without deep training or a spiritual gift.

were eliminated in 1905, Zhū Xī's interpretations continue to color the way many people read the *Four Books*, even today.[11]

Zhū Xī is a figure in the movement known in the West as "Neo-Confucianism." Neo-Confucianism, which came to intellectual maturity during the Song dynasty (960–1279 CE), sought to revive and reinvigorate the teachings of Confucianism after centuries of Buddhist dominance in the Six Dynasties Period (220–581 CE) and the Tang dynasty (618–906 CE). Although the Neo-Confucians were officially anti-Buddhist, they absorbed many concepts from Buddhism and unconsciously reinterpreted their own tradition in the light of these concepts. I like to say that Neo-Confucianism is Confucianism seen through Buddhist lenses.[12]

9.4.3. A More Prosaic Interpretation of *Analects* 5.13

Zhū Xī accepts a tradition that Kǒngzǐ wrote the "Appended Remarks" to the *Classic of Changes* (易經 Yìjīng, often called the *I Ching* in English, following the Wade-Giles romanization). The "Appended Remarks" sketches a metaphysics based on 陰 yīn and 陽 yáng, complementary aspects of the Pattern of the universe. *Yin* is manifested in things that

---

11. Nerd note: When I say "literally memorize all of the *Four Books* and Zhū Xī's commentary on them," you probably assume I mean "memorize lots of" them. I do not. By "literally memorize all" I mean literally memorize *all*. If this seems impossible for you to believe, it is because you have been raised in a culture whose attitude toward the written word has changed due to the printing press, then radio, then television, and now the internet. On Zhū Xī's educational revolution, see Daniel Gardner, *The Four Books: The Basic Teachings of the Later Confucian Tradition* (Indianapolis: Hackett Publishing, 2007), especially pp. xiii–xxx, 131–47.

12. For readings from Chinese Buddhist and Neo-Confucian texts, see Justin Tiwald and Bryan W. Van Norden, eds., *Readings in Later Chinese Philosophy* (Indianapolis: Hackett Publishing, 2011). "Neo-Confucianism" is not a direct translation of any one Chinese expression. In Chinese, the movement is known by various expressions with different connotations, including 道學 Dàoxué, "Learning of the Way," and 宋明儒學 Sōng-Míng Rúxué, "Song-Ming [Dynasties] Confucianism."

are dark, passive, falling, moist, feminine, etc., while *yang* is manifested in things that are light, active, rising, dry, masculine, etc. The "Appended Remarks" explains that "the alternation of *yin* and *yang* is called the 'Way.' That which ensues from it is goodness, and that which realizes it completely is human nature."[13]

Now, discussions of yin-yang metaphysics are conspicuously absent from the *Analects*. *Analects* 7.17 is the only passage that makes even a passing reference to the *Classic of Changes*, and Kǒngzǐ does not claim there to have written any part of the *Changes*.[14] Furthermore, the only passage in the *Analects* where Kǒngzǐ himself says anything about human nature is the one we read in Lesson 1, and he was pretty vague there. Zhū Xī explains this inconsistency by claiming that Kǒngzǐ had esoteric teachings that were only recorded for posterity in the "Appended Remarks" to the *Changes*. Consequently, when Zǐgòng says in 5.13 that "One cannot get to hear the Master discuss [human] nature and the Way of Heaven!" Zhū Xī interprets this as Zǐgòng's exclamation of joy when he finally *has* gotten to hear the topics the master "seldom spoke of." (As an analogy, imagine someone eating a perfectly prepared cut of filet mignon and exclaiming, "You *cannot* get steaks this good anymore!" Well, obviously you *can* get steaks that good, because you're eating one now, but we know what you mean.)

Zhū Xī's interpretation is brilliant (as always), but there is a simpler explanation. Maybe the reason why the content and style of the "Appended Remarks" seem so different from the *Analects* is that former does not record Kǒngzǐ's own teachings. There is actually no real evidence that Kǒngzǐ wrote the "Appended Remarks." If we take this possibility seriously, Zǐgòng's comments in 5.13 can be read in a much more straightforward way. When he says, "One cannot get to hear the Master discuss

---

13. Tiwald and Van Norden, *Readings in Later Chinese Philosophy*, pp. 46–47.
14. There is also an alternative interpretation of the passage according to which it does not refer to the *Changes* at all. See Ivanhoe and Van Norden, *Readings in Classical Chinese Philosophy*, p. 22.

[human] nature and the Way of Heaven," he means that one cannot get to hear the Master discuss human nature and the Way of Heaven—because those were topics the Master was not particularly interested in and did not talk about.

Free practice materials—including quizzes and additional readings—are available at www.hackettpublishing.com/chinese-for-everyone-support.

Lesson 10

10.1. Reading: Zhuāngzǐ and Huìzǐ Debate by the River Hao

莊子與惠子遊於濠梁之上。莊子曰。鯈魚出遊從容是魚樂也。惠子曰。子非魚。安知魚之樂。莊子曰。子非我。安知我不知魚之樂。惠子曰。我非子。固不知子矣。子固非魚也。子之不知魚之樂全矣。莊子曰。請循其本。子曰。汝安知魚樂云者。既已知吾知之而問我。我知之濠上也。

10.2. Vocabulary

Character	Hint	Pronunciation	Relevant Meaning
莊 (庄)		Zhuāng	n., Zhuāng (family name [姓] of a great Daoist philosopher; 名周。字子休。)
惠		Huì	n., Huì (family name of a philosopher known for his clever arguments; 名施。)
遊	radical + 9 strokes		
濠		Háo	濠。水名也。[1]
梁	radical + 7 strokes		
上	radical + 2 strokes		
儵	radical + 7 strokes		
魚 (鱼)	(no hint)		
從容		cōngróng	s.v., to be easygoing
子		zǐ	n., you (honorific second-person pronoun; contrast 汝 rǔ)
安		ān	adv., how . . .? from where . . .?
我	radical + 3 strokes		
請 (请)	radical + 8 strokes		
循	radical + 9 strokes		
云 者		yún zhě	exp., was said (used to mark the end of a quotation or paraphrase)
全	radical + 4 strokes		
既	radical + 5 strokes		
已		yǐ	已者既也。[2]

1. Nerd note: This definition is from the 經典釋文 Jīngdiǎn shìwén, *Explanations of the Texts of the Classics* by 陸德明 Lù Démíng of the Tang dynasty (618–906 CE).
2. In other words, 已 yǐ has a new meaning in this passage (in addition to "to stop"), and that new meaning is the same as 既, which you should look up in the dictionary.

10.3. Grammar Notes

Dictionary Practice, Some Common Radicals, Reduplicative
Expressions, Coordination of Verbs without Conjunctions, More
on Dropping 也 yě, Embedded Quotations with 云 yún

This passage is from the 莊子 *Zhuāngzǐ*, a work named after its author,
who lived in the fourth century BCE (姓莊。名周。字子休。).[3] The
Zhuāngzǐ is one of the two classics of Daoism. Westerners who are famil-
iar with Daoism have usually heard only of the *Dào dé jīng*, attributed to
Lǎozǐ. However, many of those who have read both texts believe that the
Zhuāngzǐ is by far the more profound and beautiful work. It is certainly one
of the greatest literary and philosophical texts the world has ever known.

10.3.1. Dictionary Practice

The reading in this lesson is a lot of fun, but I am going to make you
work a little to get to the entertainment. You are going to do an exercise
to learn how to look up characters in a traditional Chinese dictionary.
Fortunately, there are not too many new characters in this lesson. In addi-
tion, I'll give you some of the characters for free and provide hints for the
characters you need to look up.

Recall from the Introduction that a traditional dictionary like the
康熙字典 *Kāngxī zìdiǎn* groups characters according to their radi-
cals plus the number of strokes in addition to the radical. There are 214
Kāngxī radicals, and every Chinese character has at least one radical, or
the character is itself the radical. Sometimes the radical is not obvious, or

---

3. Nerd note: The *Zhuāngzǐ* is divided into three sections: Inner Chapters,
Outer Chapters, and Miscellaneous Chapters. One common view is that the
Inner Chapters (1–7) are by the historical Zhuāngzǐ, while the Outer and Mis-
cellaneous Chapters are by other authors, who vary greatly in their literary qual-
ities and philosophical depth. The reading in this lesson is from 秋水 Qiūshuǐ,
"Autumn Floods," which is one of the Outer Chapters. For an English transla-
tion, see Ivanhoe and Van Norden, *Readings in Classical Chinese Philosophy*,
p. 247. For more readings from "Autumn Floods," see Rouzer, Unit 6, pp. 307–62.

it looks different in the character from its stand-alone form. Below, there is a chart that shows the ten most common radicals, some additional radicals you need to know to look up the characters in this lesson, and some decoy radicals (ones easy to mistake for the ones you need). If there are significant alternative forms of the radical I also provide that. Remember that, in using a dictionary, part of what you need to do is to figure out which of the meanings listed is the relevant one for the text you are reading. In choosing a dictionary, make sure you use one that focuses on, or at least includes, *Classical* Chinese expressions. I recommend using one of the following, with the best at the top.

Kroll, Paul W. *A Student's Dictionary of Classical and Medieval Chinese.* Rev. ed. Brill, 2017. This is now the best dictionary for Classical Chinese. The index to characters by radicals is on pp. 655–714. This is also available as a paid add-on to the *Pleco Chinese Dictionary* phone app.

Liang Shih-ch'iu, ed. *Far East Chinese-English Dictionary.* 20th ed. Far East Book Company, 1999. For many years, this was my go-to desk dictionary. The main entries are arranged by radicals, but there is also a radical index and a pronunciation index.

Mathews, Robert H. *Mathews Chinese-English Dictionary.* Rev. ed. Harvard University Press, 1966. This is what people used back in the day. It is organized according to Wade-Giles romanization.

羅竹風 Luó Zhúfēng, ed., 漢語大辭典 *Hànyǔ dà cídiǎn* (*Comprehensive Dictionary of Chinese*), multiple editions and formats. Whereas the previous three dictionaries are Chinese-English dictionaries, this one is a Chinese–Chinese dictionary. This is the Chinese equivalent of the *Oxford English Dictionary*. You should know that this work exists, because it is what serious Sinologists use when they want an authoritative answer about the use of a character or expression. However, if you could use the *Hànyǔ dà cídiǎn*, you wouldn't be reading this book, would you?

10.3.2. Some Common Radicals

Official Radical	Alternative Forms	English Nickname	Strokes in Radical
一		one	1
亠		lid	2
人	亻	person/standing man	2
入		enter	2
冫		ice	2
口		mouth	3
女		woman	3
宀		roof	3
夂		stride	3
彳		two-headed man	3
心	忄	heart/standing heart	4
戈		lance	4
手	扌	hand/side hand	4
无		not	4
木		tree	4
水	氵	water/three-dots water	4
火	灬	fire/four-dots fire	4
牙		fang	4
竹		bamboo	6
肉	月	meat	6
艸	艹	grass	6
糸	纟	silk	6
虫		insect	6
言		speech	7
辵	辶	walk	7
魚		fish	11

10.3.3. Reduplicative Expressions

In Classical Chinese most words are represented by one character, but there are some binomes (two-character expressions for one word).[4] One kind is the reduplicative binome, in which two words that rhyme combine to form a word describing the style or manner of something. (Compare "helter-skelter" or "willy-nilly" in English.) In this lesson, we find 從容 cōngróng, a stative verb meaning "to be carefree."[5]

10.3.4. Coordination of Verbs without Conjunctions

This lesson gives us an example of parataxis, the coordination of expressions without explicit conjunctions, which we first discussed in Lesson 6. In this lesson, we have the complex expression, 出遊從容 chū yóu cōngróng in which three distinct verbs are written together without the conjunction 而 ér. Each verb functions separately: "to go out [and] 遊 [and] be carefree."

10.3.5. More on Dropping 也 yě

In Lesson 9, we saw that the final 也 yě can drop off in an affirmative N1 N2 也 construction. In this lesson, we see that the same thing can happen with a negative nominal sentence:

N1 非 N2 也 → N1 非 N2
N1 is not an N2

子非魚也。 → 子非魚。
You, sir, are not a fish.

---

4. Nerd note: Modern Chinese has far more multi-character expressions. For example, in the transition from Classical to Modern Chinese, 雖 becomes 雖然, 如 becomes 如果, 知 becomes 知道, and 自 and 己 merge into 自己. In Modern Chinese we even find delightful polysyllabic expressions like 唯物主義者 wéiwùzhǔyìzhě, "materialist" (literally, only-thing-dominant-meaning-ist).

5. Nerd note: Remember that just because two words rhyme in Modern Chinese that does not mean that they rhymed in Classical Chinese. However, these two words did. Incidentally, most dictionaries read 從容 as cóngróng, but I am following Kroll (p. 66) and giving the pronunciation as cōngróng.

10.3.6. Embedded Quotations with 云 yún

Sometimes 云 yún works like our old friend 曰 yuē and just means "said." However, it often is used when what is said is a quotation within a quotation, especially someone quoting a classic text. 云 yún can also occur at the end of a clause, where it may indicate that the preceding expression is a paraphrase or hypothetical (rather than a direct quotation). In this last use, it can combine with other grammatical particles like 云爾 yún ěr, or 云者 yún zhě.

Pattern:

> N1 曰。 N2 云 ……
> N1 said that N2 said that . . .
>
> P 。 N1云。
> N1 said that P.
>
> N1 曰 P 云者。
> N1 said something like P.

Examples:

> 曾子曰。子云。好之不如樂之。
> Zēngzǐ said, "The Master said, 'being fond of it is not as good as delighting in it.'"
>
> 其子亦云。
> His son also said that. ["That" refers to something expressed in an earlier sentence.]
>
> 禮云禮云何謂也。
> When we talk about "the rites this" and "the rites that," what do we mean?

10.4. Supplement
10.4.1. Philosophy or Sophistry?

We saw in Lesson 3 that 安 ān can mean "peace" or "to regard as peaceful." In this lesson, we learn that it can also mean "How . . .?" and "From where . . .?" Zhuāngzǐ's final rebuttal to Huizi depends upon the ambiguity between these two last senses. Huizi begins by questioning *how* Zhuāngzǐ could know something (suggesting that there is no way he could know it), but Zhuāngzǐ intentionally misinterprets Huizi as asking *where* Zhuāngzǐ got his knowledge.

I'm sure this reading gave you a smile, but is there anything more to it than a clever sophistry made possible by a pun? 郭慶藩 Guō Qìngfān, a commentator of the Qing dynasty (1644–1911), suggested that Zhuāngzǐ was trying to teach Huizi that, even though the "myriad things" of the world are different and have their own natures, we can understand the common Pattern (理 lǐ) that they all share and thereby sympathize with their feelings. (See Lesson 9 on "Pattern.") Huizi can know what Zhuāngzǐ knows, but for that same reason Zhuāngzǐ can know what fish know. And Huizi could know what fish know too, if he would only try.[6]

We'll read another passage from Zhuāngzǐ in Lesson 13, and it will teach a similar lesson about the unity of things.

Free practice materials—including quizzes and additional readings—are available at www.hackettpublishing.com/chinese-for-everyone-support.

---

6. For an excellent discussion of this passage, see John R. Williams, "Two Paradigmatic Strategies for Reading Zhuang Zi's 'Happy Fish' Vignette as Philosophy," *Comparative Philosophy* 9:2 (2018): 93–104.

Lesson 11

11.1. Readings: Two Poems by Lǐ Bái: "Thoughts on a Still Night" and "Expressing My Feelings When Waking Up from Being Drunk on a Spring Day"

處世若大夢。
胡爲勞其生。
所以終日醉。
頹然臥前楹。

床前明月光。
疑是地上霜。
舉頭望明月。
低頭思故鄉。

11.2. Vocabulary

(Twenty-six new characters, six new uses)

床 chuáng n., bed (but see supplement 11.4.2)

前 qián n., the front

明 míng s.v., to be bright; s.v., to be enlightened

月 yuè n., moon

光 guāng s.v., to shine

疑 yí t.v., to suspect that, to wonder whether

地 dì n., earth; ground

霜 shuāng n., frost

舉 (举) jǔ t.v., to lift

頭 (头) tóu n., head

望 wàng t.v., to look at

低 dī t.v., to lower

思 sī t.v., to think longingly of

故鄉 (故乡) gùxiāng n., hometown (literally, old town)

世 shì n., world; n., era

若 ruò s.v., to be like

大 dà s.v., to be big

夢 (梦) mèng n., dream

胡為 hú wèi exp., for what (reason)

勞 (劳) láo t.v., to belabor, to make work for

生 shēng n., life

所以 suǒyǐ conj., because of this, therefore

終日 zhōngrì adv., all day (literally, end day)

醉 zuì s.v., to be intoxicated

頹 (颓) tuí s.v., to slump, to sprawl

然 rán g.p., -ingly (follows a stative verb, converting it into an adverb); s.v., to be so, to be this way

臥 wò s.v., to sleep

楹 yíng n., pillar (here refers to the pillars at the front of his house's entrance hall)

11.3. Grammar Notes

Introducing 所以 suǒyǐ, Changing Stative Verbs to Adverbs with 然 rán, Four Reminders

With this lesson, we are jumping forward a thousand years to learn two pieces of poetry by 李白 Lǐ Bái (701–762 CE), one of the greatest poets of Chinese history. The first poem is 靜夜思 Jìng yè sī, "Thoughts on a Still Night." The second piece is the first of the three stanzas of 春日醉起 言志 Chūn rì zuì qǐ yán zhì, "Expressing My Feelings When Waking Up from Being Drunk on a Spring Day." In the interests of not overwhelming you with new characters, I have only given you the first of three stanzas in the reading, but see supplement 11.4.3 below for the rest.

11.3.1. Introducing 所以 suǒyǐ

We know that 所 suǒ can precede a transitive verb, converting it into a phrase describing the object of the verb (Lesson 7) and we know that 以 yǐ can be a verb meaning "by means of" (Lesson 6). If we put these meanings together, we see that 所以 must mean "that by means of which." In later Chinese, as in this lesson, the phrase means more specifically "therefore."[1]

11.3.2. Changing Stative Verbs to Adverbs with 然 rán

In Lesson 8, we saw that 然 rán can be a stative verb meaning "is so" or "is this way." In this lesson, we see another common use, in which 然 follows a stative verb and converts it into an adverb. I suggest as a literal translation for this lesson -ingly (as in "slump-ingly"), but as Kroll observes this word "needs to be rendered *ad hoc* according to context" (p. 383).

---

1. Nerd note: For examples of other uses, see Kroll, pp. 437–38.

11.3.3. Four Reminders

The rest of the grammar of these poems is not too hard, as long as you remember a few things we have already learned. First, a 之 zhī can drop out between two nouns.

N1 之 N2 → N1 N2
the N2 of N1

Second, remember that a stative verb in front of a noun can act as an adjective.

SV N
an N that is SV

Third, don't forget that 是 shì in Classical Chinese is a pronoun meaning "this" (typically referring back to something discussed earlier).

N1。 是 N2 也。
N1. This is N2.

Finally, remember that the 也 can drop off of a nominal sentence.

N1 N2 也 → N1 N2.
N1 is N2.

11.4. Supplements
11.4.1. Author and Style

The two poems in this lesson are in a style that has stanzas of four lines of five syllables each (some poems of this style have seven syllables per line), and after the first two characters of each line there is a caesura (a pause that typically marks a syntactic break).[2] The author, Lǐ Bái, is generally

---

2. Nerd note: There is a complicated system for classifying Chinese poems according to the number of lines, the number of syllables in each line, the rhyme scheme, and also the pattern of tones. Both of the poems in this lesson are "five-syllable ancient style" (五言古詩 wǔ yán gǔ shī). Traditionally, 靜夜思 is categorized as an example of five-syllable regulated verse (五言絕句 wǔ yán jué jù), but it does not have the right tone pattern for this style.

considered one of the two greatest Chinese poets, along with 杜甫 Dù Fǔ.[3] Both lived during the Tang dynasty (618–906 CE). If you want to impress people at a cocktail party, say that Lǐ Bái is a "Daoist" poet whose works deal with the joys of drinking wine and appreciating the beauty of nature, while Dù Fǔ is a "Confucian" poet whose works are often lamentations on the sad state of the world. However, if you run into someone who knows that those are grotesque oversimplifications of multifaceted geniuses, just switch the conversation to what you're watching on Netflix.

静夜思 Jìng yè sī is the single most famous poem in all of Chinese history, and almost every literate Chinese person has memorized it. (So you should memorize it too. Try reciting it to Chinese friends and watch the reaction you get.) Like any work that captures the collective imagination of a particular culture, outsiders may initially have trouble appreciating its depth. However, it is extremely evocative for those steeped in traditional Chinese thought and literature. It conjures an image of a person who is far from home, probably on a journey required by his obligations to his family or his ruler. We intensely feel his longing for his home, yet the expression of emotions is as cool as the frost-like light of the moon on the ground. The moon is an extremely common figure in Chinese (and Japanese) poetry. Part of the test of a poet is whether he can invoke the moon in a way that seems fresh rather than trite. In this poem, Lǐ Bái simultaneously makes use of different associations of the moon: the moon as one's companion, the moon as what links one to loved ones far away (because we look at the same moon), the moon as austere and mysterious.

春日醉起言志 Chūn rì zuì qǐ yán zhì is one of many poems in which Lǐ Bái emphasizes the joys of drinking wine. The poem might seem to be a degenerate account of getting drunk, but 醉 zuì can refer to a variety of states from being slightly tipsy to "full-on wasty pants." Lǐ Bái envisions the effect of the wine as helping to silence the artificial aspects of the self and bring him more in touch with his true, spontaneous self and the natural world.

---

3. Nerd note: 李白 Lǐ Bái is traditionally referred to in English as "Li Po." This is because very old-fashioned people read 白 with the 讀音 dúyīn (Lesson 3.3.3) of Bó, and in Wade-Giles "Bo" is written "Po."

11.4.2. On Beds

The character 床 chuáng typically means "bed," and that makes sense in this context. (Imagine someone in bed looking at the moonlight as it comes through the window and shines on the floor.) However, the same word can refer to a railing around a well, and there are also some interpreters who think this character is a mistake for 窗 chuāng, which means "window."

11.4.3. The Rest of "Expressing My Feelings When Waking Up from Being Drunk on a Spring Day" 春日醉起言志

You can use a dictionary to read the rest of the poem. Here are the second and third stanzas (with a few hints, because I am nice like that).

覺來眄庭前。	來 lái, g.p. (follows V and indicates change of status)
一鳥花間鳴。	
借問此何時。	借問 jiè wèn, exp., I took the occasion to ask, so I said
春風語流鶯。	流鶯 liú yīng, exp., melodious oriole, sweet-singing bird
感之慾嘆息。	
對酒還自傾。	還 huán, v., to return to, to resume
浩歌待明月。	
曲盡已忘情。	

Free practice materials—including quizzes and additional readings—are available at www.hackettpublishing.com/chinese-for-everyone-support.

Lesson 12

12.1. Readings: *Mèngzǐ* 2A6, 7B3 (Edited)

孟子曰。所以謂人皆有不忍人之心者。今人乍見孺子將入於井。皆有怵惕惻隱之心。非人也。惻隱之心。仁之端也。苟能充之。苟不充之，足以保四海。苟不充之，不足以事父母。

孟子曰。盡信書。則不如無書。

12.2. Vocabulary

(Twenty-four new characters, four new uses)

孟 Mèng n., Meng (family name [姓] of a great Confucian philosopher; 名軻。)

所以 suǒyǐ n., that by means of which, the reason why; conj., because of this, therefore

忍 rěn t.v., to be unfeeling toward[1]

今 jīn g.p. (indicates counterfactual mood)

乍 zhà adv., suddenly

見 (见) jiàn t.v., to see; xiàn, s.v., to be visible

孺子 rúzǐ n. baby; n., toddler

將 jiāng v., will, shall, going to

入 rù s.v., to enter (here, it implies falling)

井 jǐng n., well

怵惕 chùtì n., alarm, fear

惻隱 (恻隐) cèyǐn n., sympathy, compassion

心 xīn n. heart; n. feeling

端 duān n. tip; n. sprout (but see supplement 12.4.2)

苟 gǒu conj., if only

能 néng v., to be able to

充 chōng t.v., to fill up; t.v., to make complete

足 zú s.v., to be sufficient

保 bǎo t.v., to protect

四海 sì hǎi n., the Four Seas; n., the inhabited world

事 shì t.v., to serve (especially a superior)

盡 (尽) jìn adv., wholly, completely, fully

信 xìn t.v., to have faith in, to have confidence in, to believe in; adv., truly, genuinely

書 shū n., the *Documents*; n., book, writings

---

1. The characters for *ninja* in Japanese are 忍者, meaning "those who are ruthless."

12.3. Grammar Notes

Modal 今 jīn, Coverb 將 jiāng, the *Documents* 書 Shū

This reading consists of two passages, both from the eponymous *Mèngzǐ* (孟子 Mèngzǐ). Mèngzǐ (姓孟。名軻。) was an older contemporary of Zhuāngzǐ; both lived in the fourth century BCE. The first selection is part of the famous story of the "child at the well" (*Mèngzǐ* 2A6), and the second is Mèngzǐ's comment on textual authority (7B3).[2] Passages in the *Mèngzǐ* are identified by their book (there are seven "books," each the length of a chapter), the part of the book (上 and 下 in Chinese, but "A" and "B" in English), and the individual section or "chapter."

12.3.1. Modal 今 jīn

今 jīn can mean "now" (as in the Modern Chinese 今天 jīntiān, "today," and 今年 jīnnián, "this year"). However, in this reading we see a modal use of 今 that introduces a counterfactual: "Suppose that . . ." or "If it were the case that . . ." 今 can also mark a slight change in topic. Compare the English use of "now" in phrases like "Now, I ain't a betting man, but if I was. . . ."

12.3.2. Coverb 將 jiāng

將 jiāng combines with another verb to indicate that the action of the second verb will occur in the future, or that the verb expresses the intention of the agent of the verb. In English, you will often express these meanings with verbs like "will," "shall," or "going to."

12.3.3. The *Documents* 書 Shū

The word 書 shū can mean "writings", "documents" (in a generic sense), or "books." It can also mean "to write" (which is now its primary meaning in

---

2. For English translations, see Ivanhoe and Van Norden, *Readings in Classical Chinese Philosophy,* pp. 129–30, 154–55.

Japanese). However, in Classical Chinese it is often the name of a particular work, the *Documents* (also called the *Classic of Documents* 書經 Shūjīng). During the Han dynasty (202 BCE–220 CE), the *Documents* became one of the *Five Classics* (五經 Wǔjīng, not to be confused with the *Four Books*), along with the *Odes* (詩 Shī), *Changes* (易 Yì), *Spring and Autumn Annals* (春秋 Chūnqiū), and *Record of Rites* (禮記 Lǐjì). These books were the basis of Confucian higher education until the educational reforms of Zhū Xī (see Lesson 9.4.2).

12.4. Supplements
12.4.1. Author and Philosophy

Mèngzǐ is called the "Second Sage" (亞聖 yàshèng) of Confucianism, second in importance only to Kǒngzǐ himself. He is best known for his claim that 性善 xìng shàn, "[human] nature is good." The *Mèngzǐ*, the collection of his sayings and dialogues with others, became one of the *Four Books* of the Confucian canon.

In 2A6, Mèngzǐ presents what Western philosophers call a "thought experiment" in order to convince us that human nature is good. He asks us to imagine what feelings we think any normal human would have in a particular situation. He hopes that reflection upon this scenario will lead us to see that compassion is part of what it is to be a human being. A sociopath who lacked compassion is more an animal than a human. As another of the *Four Books* says, 仁者人也 rén zhě rén yě, "Benevolence is being a human."[3]

Mèngzǐ's thought experiment is carefully crafted. He does not claim that anyone who saw the child at the well would act to save the child. He only claims that they would have a certain "feeling" (literally, "heart"). He says that this innate feeling is merely the "sprout" (or "tip") of the virtue of benevolence. We must "complete it" (literally, "fill it up") in order to be fully virtuous. If we fail to do so, we will not even be able to reliably care for our own parents.

---

3. The *Mean*, chapter 20.

In 7B3, Mèngzǐ warns us against the dangers of uncritically accepting the classics. In the rest of this passage and in other parts of his text, he makes clear that we have to interpret texts contextually and creatively, rather than rigidly and literally.

12.4.2. The Controversy over 端 duān

In his commentary on this passage,[4] Zhū Xī says,

端緒也。……猶有物在中而緒見於外也。

緒 xù, n., tip, end point

猶 yóu, v., to be like, to be similar to

However, an alternative interpretation is that 端 is a scribal miscopying for 耑 duān, which is a pictogram of a sprout breaking through the soil. The justification for this reading is that Mèngzǐ frequently appeals to agricultural metaphors to explain ethical cultivation, and he uses several different terms for sprouts in other passages.[5] Which do you think is the correct reading and why?

12.4.3. Which "Four Seas"?

A common view in ancient China was that the Heavens are round and the Earth is square. The land of the Earth was thought to be surrounded by water on all sides, so this led to the expression "the Four Seas" 四海 Sìhǎi (one for each compass direction). By association, this expression came to refer to the whole inhabited world.

---

4. If you don't remember what commentary I'm talking about or who Zhū Xī is, shame on you. But see Lesson 9.

5. Also remember the principle of *lectio difficilior* (Lesson 6).

12.4.4. Mèngzǐ's Critics

Although Mèngzǐ was very influential, he had his opponents.[6] The later Confucian 荀子 Xúnzǐ criticized Mèngzǐ by name, arguing that, contrary to what Mèngzǐ claimed, "human nature is bad," 性惡 xìng è. Mèngzǐ's contemporary Zhuāngzǐ never mentions him explicitly, but it is clear that many passages in the *Zhuāngzǐ* are critiques of Mèngzǐ's views. For example, in the rest of *Mèngzi* 2A6, he claims that we not only have an innate 仁之端, but also an innate 義之端 (sprout of righteousness) and a 是非之心 (feeling of right and wrong). Zhuāngzǐ seems to be criticizing this view when he writes:[7]

仁義之端。是非之途。樊然殽亂。

Rén yì zhī duān, shì fēi zhī tú, fánrán xiáo luàn.

仁義 rén yì n., benevolence and righteousness
是非 shì fēi n., approval and disapproval, right and wrong
途 tú n., path
樊然 fánrán, adv., confusingly
殽 xiáo s.v., to be jumbled
亂 luàn s.v., to be chaotic

Free practice materials—including quizzes and additional readings—are available at www.hackettpublishing.com/chinese-for-everyone-support.

---

6. Nerd note: For discussions of all their views, see Bryan W. Van Norden, *Introduction to Classical Chinese Philosophy* (Indianapolis: Hackett Publishing, 2011). For more Chinese selections from the *Mengzi*, see Rouzer, Unit 4, pp. 227–78.
7. *Zhuangzi* 2. See Ivanhoe and Van Norden, *Readings in Classical Chinese Philosophy*, p. 222 for a translation.

Lesson 13

13.1. Reading: The Butterfly Dream from the *Zhuāngzǐ*

昔者莊周夢為胡蝶。栩栩然

胡蝶也。自喻適志與。不知

周也。俄然覺。則蘧蘧然周

也。不知周之夢為胡蝶與。

胡蝶之夢為周與。周與胡蝶

。則必有分矣。此之謂物化。

13.2. Vocabulary

(Fifteen new characters, six new uses)

昔 者 xī zhě adv., in the past, once upon a time

周 Zhōu n., Zhōu (personal name [名] of a great Daoist
   philosopher; 姓莊。字子休。)

夢 (梦) mèng t.v., to dream (that); n., dream

胡蝶 húdíe n., butterfly

栩栩 xǔxǔ s.v., to be lively

喻 yù t.v., to understand

適 shì t.v., to satisfy

志 zhì n., intentions, goals

與 (与) yú g.p. (sentence-final exclamatory); yǔ conj., and
   (joins nouns); yú g.p. (sentence-final interrogative)

俄 é s.v., to be sudden

覺 (觉) jué s.v., to be conscious

則 (则) zé conj., then; g.p. (contrastive topic marker)

蘧蘧 qúqú s.v., to be sudden

必 bì adv., must, necessarily

分 fēn n., distinction

此 cǐ n., this

之謂 zhī wèi exp., is what is called

化 huà n., transformation

13.3. Grammar Notes

Our final reading is one of the most famous passages in all of Chinese lit-
erature: the story of the butterfly dream from chapter 2 of the *Zhuāngzǐ*.[1]

---

1. For an English translation, see Ivanhoe and Van Norden, *Readings in Classical
Chinese Philosophy*, p. 224.

13.3.1. Names Used in the First Person

If I were to say, "Bryan has been teaching you Classical Chinese. Bryan is proud of you for making it to the final lesson in this book," you'd think I was painfully full of myself (and probably full of something else too). But in Classical Chinese it is perfectly polite and idiomatic to refer to yourself by your own name.[2] Consequently, the proper translation of the opening line of this reading could be "Once, Zhuang Zhou dreamed that he was . . . ," but (since this is a book attributed to Zhuang Zhou) it could also be, "Once, I dreamed that I was. . . ."

13.3.2. The Many Senses of 與 yǔ/yú

We see several different uses of 與 yú/yú in this passage. First, it is simply an exclamatory grammatical particle (yú). Next, it is used as paired interrogative particles to mark an alternative (yú):

> P1與。 P2 與。
> Is it P1? Or is it P2?

Finally, it is being used as a simple conjunction (yǔ, from Lesson 7).

13.3.3. The Archaism 之謂 zhī wèi

謂 wèi, "to call [so-and-so] [such-and-such]," takes a direct and an indirect object (what is being called and what it is called). So what we would expect in Classical Chinese (and what we do find in some texts) is

Pattern:

> 謂 N1 N2
> to call N1 "N2"

Example:

> 吾必謂之學矣。
> I would definitely call him learned.[3]

---

2. The same is true of Modern Chinese and Japanese.
3. *Analects* 2.7.

But there is also a way of expressing this that is an archaism (a fossil of pre-Classical Chinese that survives into Classical):[4]

Pattern:

N1 之謂 N2

N1 is what is meant by "N2."

Example:

天命之謂性。

What is mandated by Heaven is what is meant by "nature."[5]

This archaism is typically used when the author wants to give a definitive statement about what something is.

13.4. Supplements

13.4.1. Philosophy: Skepticism or Monism?

This story ends on a note of uncertainty about whether Zhuāngzǐ is dreaming or not. This has led some interpreters to compare it to the dream argument of French philosopher René Descartes (1596–1650). Descartes considered the possibility that all of his specific beliefs about the world might be mistaken, because he could merely be dreaming that he is awake, sitting by the fire, writing a book, etc. The goal of Descartes' philosophy was to find a way to *escape* this uncertainty by finding an indubitable foundation for knowledge.

In contrast, Zhuāngzǐ's butterfly dream is about *embracing* the ambiguity of identity. Elsewhere in the Inner Chapters, Zhuāngzǐ writes that the "ancient sages . . . slept calmly and woke blankly. Sometimes they took themselves for horses. Sometimes they took themselves for cows."[6] So Zhuāngzǐ is not bemoaning the fact that we cannot tell what the truth is. He is taking delight in the fact that in awakening from a dream he has

---

4. Nerd note: For more on this archaism, see Pulleyblank, VIII.1, pp. 70–71. On 謂 in general see Pulleyblank, IV.8f, pp. 33–34.

5. Nerd note: The *Mean*, chapter 1.

6. Ivanhoe and Van Norden, *Readings*, p. 242.

gotten a glimpse of what the world looks like to a true sage, for whom everything is one.

13.4.2. Controversy over 喻 yù

The character 喻 yù means "to understand." Consequently, the received text of this passage seems to say that, when he was dreaming that he was a butterfly, Zhuāngzǐ 自喻 zì yù, "understood himself" (as a butterfly). This is how the Qing dynasty commentator 郭慶藩 Guō Qìngfān understands it. However, the Six Dynasties (220–581 CE) commentator 郭象 Guó Xiàng thinks that 喻 is a miscopying for 豫 yù, "to be content." This would give us the meaning 自豫, "happy with himself."

13.4.3. On 物化 wù huà

Recognizing that the butterfly dream is not a skeptical argument takes us a step toward understanding what Zhuāngzǐ means by describing it as 物化 wù huà, "the transformation of things." In the *Zhuāngzǐ*, 化 huà describes the continuous process of change of the natural world, in which there are no precise boundaries between one state and another. There are no absolute distinctions in the transformation of the living into the dead, or of a caterpillar into a butterfly. So in not clearly distinguishing between himself and a butterfly, Zhuāngzǐ has a more accurate perception of the world.

此書已矣。學則不已。
學則不已。不亦樂乎。

Glossary

Characters are ordered by their total number of strokes, then by lesson of first occurrence; compound expressions may be found under the first character.

1

一 yi (pronounced yī alone, changes to yí in front of a syllable with a fourth tone, changes to yì in front of any other tone) n., one L8

2

人 rén n., others, other people L3; n., people, persons L7

力 lì n., strength, power L4

入 rù s.v., to enter L12

3

子 zǐ n., the Master L1; n., -master (honorific following a family name); n., son; s.v., to be a son, to act as a son (should) L2; n., daughter L6; n. you (honorific second-person pronoun) L10

子貢 Zǐgòng n., Zigong (style [字] of a disciple of Kǒngzǐ; 姓端木。名賜。) L8

也 yě g.p. (comes at end of sentences to mark nominal sentences; often indicates a generalization) L1; 也 yě g.p. (vocative particle—follows name of person addressed) L8

山 shān n., mountains L3

之 zhī n., him, her, them, it (third-person pronoun, must be the object of a verb or preposition) L4; g.p., (subordinates one nominal phrase to another, showing possession or specification) L6

之謂 zhī wèi exp., is what is called L13

士 shì n., aristocrat, scholar, warrior L7

己 jǐ n., self, oneself (can be used to attributively of nouns) L7

已 yǐ s.v., to stop L7

巳 sì n., sixth of the twelve Earthly Branches (part of a traditional calendrical system); contrast 己 jǐ, oneself, and 已 yǐ, to stop) L7 (supplement)

上 L10

大 dà s.v., to be big L11

4

曰 yuē v., to say (used to introduce a direct quotation; contrast 日 rì) L1

公 gōng n., duke (highest hereditary title below the king) L2

公冶 Gōngyě n., Gongye (a two-syllable family name, literally "Duke's Smelter" or "Dukesmith") L6

孔 Kǒng n., Kong (the family name [姓] of 孔子 Kǒngzǐ, Master Kong, better known in the West as "Confucius"; 名丘。字仲尼。) L2

父 fù n., father; s.v., to be a father, to act as a father (should) L2

不 bù (tone changes to bú before a word in fourth tone) adv., not (negates verbs or verbal phrases) L2

不亦……乎 bú yì . . . hū exp., is it not . . .? L7

仁 rén s.v., to be fully human; s.v., to be benevolent; n., humaneness; n., benevolence L3

水 shuǐ n., water; n., rivers L3

中 zhōng n., middle, midst L6

以 yǐ v., using, taking, by means of L6

以為 yǐwéi exp., to take it as, to regard it as L7

予 yú n., I L8

勿 wù adv., do not . . . it (imperative mood) L8

夫子 Fūzǐ n., the Master L8

文章 wénzhāng n., external manifestations of a cultivated character L9

文辭 wéncí n., eloquent words L9

天 tiān n., Heaven (an impersonal higher power); s.v., to be of Heaven, Heavenly L9

日 rì adv., daily L9

云 yún v., to say (used to introduce an embedded quotation) L10

云者 yún zhě exp., was said (used to mark the end of a quotation or paraphrase) L10

月 yuè n., moon L11

今 jīn g.p. (indicates counterfactual mood) L12

井 jǐng n., well L12

心 xīn n., heart; n., feeling L12

分 fēn n., distinction L13

化 huà n., transformation L13

5

由 Yóu n., You (personal name [名] of a disciple of Kǒngzǐ; 姓 仲。字子路。) L4

乎 hū g.p. (comes at the end of a sentence, transforming it into a question; roughly like 嗎 ma in Modern Chinese) L4; g.p. (vocative particle; follows name of person addressed) L8; prep., on, from, of L9

可 kě v., can be . . .-ed L6

可以 kěyǐ v., can, may L7

母 mǔ n., mother L6

弘 hóng s.v., to be broad (metaphorically or literally) L7

去 qù t.v., to forsake, to abandon L7

出 chū s.v., to go out, to leave L8

外 wài n., the outside L9

本 běn n., root, basis; s.v., to be fundamental L9

世 shì n., world; n., era L11

生 shēng n., life L11

乍 zhà adv., suddenly L12

四海 sì hǎi n., the Four Seas; n., the inhabited world L12

必 bì adv., must, necessarily L13

6

臣 chén n., minister; s.v., to be a minister, to act as a minister (should) L2

安 ān n., peace, safety; t.v., to regard as peaceful L3; adv., how . . .? from where . . .? L10

汝 rǔ n., you (second-person singular pronoun, used to address subordinates) L4

自 zì n., self, oneself (reflexive pronoun) L4

自然 zìrán s.v., to be natural (literally, "self-so"); n., naturalness L9

有 yǒu t.v., to have L4; t.v., there is, there are, there exists L5

如 rú conj., if; t.v., to be like L5

好 hào t.v., to be fond of L5; s.v., to be good, to be pleasing L5 (note)

名 míng n., name; t.v., to give a name to L6

在 zài t.v., to be in L6

任 rèn n., responsibility L7

亦 yì g.p., (emphatic particle, indicating that something is so also, particularly, or only of the thing in question) L7

而 ér conj., and (joins verbal phrases) L7

而後 érhòu conj., and only then L7

而已矣 éryǐyǐ exp., and that is all L8

死 sǐ s.v., to die L7

多 duō adv., to do V of many things L8

行 xíng t.v., to put into effect L8

共 gòng adv., jointly, as a group L9

至於 (至于) zhìyú exp., When it comes to . . . L9

全 L10

光 guāng s.v., to shine L11

地 dì n., earth; ground L11

充 chōng t.v., to fill up; t.v., to make complete L12

此 cǐ n., this L13

7

近 jìn s.v., to be close L1

君 jūn n., ruler, lord; s.v., to be a ruler, to be a lord, to act as a ruler (should) L2

利 lì n., profit, benefit; t.v., to treat as profitable, to treat as beneficial L3

吾 wú n., I; n., my, mine L5

言 yán n., words, maxim L8; t.v., to put into words, to create maxims; t.v., to mean L9

何 hé n., what (interrogative pronoun) L8

矣 yǐ g.p., (modal particle, indicating action or state described by the verbal phrase is complete in time or degree) L8

見 (见) xiàn s.v., to be visible L9; jiàn, t.v., to see L12

罕 hǎn adv., seldom L9

我 L10

床 chuáng n., bed; n., wellhead L11

低 dī t.v., to lower L11

忍 rěn t.v., to be unfeeling toward L12

忍者 rěnzhě n., ninja L12 (note)

足 zú s.v., to be sufficient L12

志 zhì n., intentions, goals L13

8

性 xìng n., nature (as in "human nature" or "the natures of humans") L1

於 (于) yú prep., from, of L2

知 zhī t.v., to know, to understand, to appreciate; zhì n., wisdom; s.v., to be wise (N.B.: When it is a noun or a stative verb 知 is pronounced zhì, but when it is a transitive verb 知 is pronounced zhī.) L3

者 zhě g.p. (follows a verbal phrase, transforming it into a nominal phrase describing the subject of the verbal phrase: "those who . . ." or "that which . . .") L3; g.p. (transforms verbal phrase, V, into a gerund, V-ing) L5; g.p. (marks expression being defined or characterized) L9

明 míng s.v.. to be enlightened L4; s.v., to be bright L11

非 fēi v., is-not (used to negate nominal sentences) L6; s.v., to be wrong, to be mistaken L8

物 wù n., thing; n., kind of thing L6

始 shǐ n., beginning L6

長 Cháng n., Chang (a personal name) L6

妻 qì t.v., to give a wife to L6

其 qí n., his, her, its, their L6; n., the (as in "the Way," "the man") L7

其 ⋯⋯ 乎 qí . . . hū exp., Is it not . . .? (expects answer "It is . . .!") L8

所 suǒ g.p. (transforms following transitive verb into a nominal phrase describing the object of the verb) L7

所以 suǒyǐ conj., because of this, therefore L11; exp., that by means of which, the reason why L12

門人 (门人) ménrén n., disciples (literally, "gate people") L8

忠 zhōng n., loyalty, dutifulness L8

受 shòu t.v., to receive L9

固 gù adv., definitely L9

若 ruò s.v., to be like L11

臥 wò s.v., to sleep L11

孟 Mèng n., Meng (family name [姓] of a great Confucian philosopher, 孟子 Mèngzǐ, Master Meng, sometimes known in English as "Mencius"; 名軻。) L12

怵惕 chùtì n., alarm, fear L12

苟 gǒu conj., if only L12

事 shì n., to serve (especially a superior) L12

昔者 xī zhě adv., in the past, once upon a time L13

周 Zhōu n., Zhou (personal name [名] of a great Daoist philosopher, 莊子 Zhuāngzǐ, Master Zhuang; 姓莊。字子休。) L13

9

相 xiāng adv., to each other L1

政 zhèng n., government, governing L2

為 (为) wéi v., to act as L4

是 shì n., this L4

哉 zāi g.p. (exclamatory particle; usually found at the end of sentences) L5

信 xìn adv., truly, genuinely L5; t.v., to have faith in, to have confidence in, to believe in L12

食 shí t.v., to eat L5

恆 (恒) héng s.v., to be constant L6

重 zhòng s.v., to be heavy L7

怒 shù n., reciprocity, sympathy L8

施 shī t.v., to bestow something on someone (usually done by a superior to a subordinate) L8

威儀 (威仪) wēiyí n., august bearing L9

皆 jiē adv., all L9

則 (则) zé g.p., (contrastive topic marker) L9; conj., then L13

既 L10

前 qián n., the front L11

思 sī t.v., to think longingly of L11

故鄉 (故乡) gùxiāng, n., hometown (literally, old town) L11

胡為 hú wèi exp., for what (reason) L11

胡蝶 húdíe n., butterfly L13

保 bǎo t.v., to protect L12

俄 é s.v., to be sudden L13

10

莊 (庄) Zhuāng n., Zhuang (family name [姓] of a great Daoist philosopher, 莊子 Zhuāngzǐ, Master Zhuang; 名周。字子休。) L10

能 néng v., to be able to L12

書 (书) shū n., the *Documents*; n., book, writings L12

栩栩 xǔxǔ s.v., to be lively L13

11

習 (习) xí n., practices L1

問 (问) wèn t.v., to ask someone (indirect object) about something (direct object) L2; adv., questioningly, as a question L8

得 dé t.v., to get, to obtain; v., to succeed in V-ing L7

得而 dé ér exp., to succeed in V-ing L5

欲 yù t.v., to desire L7

處 (处) chǔ t.v., to dwell in, to remain in L7

貧 pín n., poverty L7

貫 (贯) guàn t.v., to bind together L8

終身 zhōngshēn exp., to the end of one's life (literally, "end self") L8

終日 zhōngrì adv., all day (literally, "end day") L11

參 (参) Shēn n., Shen (personal name [名] of a disciple of Kǒngzǐ; 姓曾。字子輿。) L8

唯 wéi v., is-so, yes (suggests prompt and unhesitating agreement) L8

理 lǐ n., Pattern, Principle L9

梁 L10

魚 L10

從容 cōngróng s.v., to be easygoing L10

望 wàng t.v., to look at L11

將 (将) jiāng v., will, shall, going to L12

12

景 jǐng s.v., to be bright, shining; n., Jing (honorific posthumous name) L2

勝 (胜) shèng t.v., to defeat, to conquer L4

强 (強) qiáng s.v., to be strong, to be powerful L4

善 shàn s.v., to be good L5

粟 sù n., grain L5

道 dào n., a path; n., a way (of living); n., the right way to follow, *the* Way; n., a linguistic account of a way; n., the metaphysical foundation of the universe; t.v., to give a linguistic account of something L6

無 (无) wú t.v., to lack, to not have L6

萬 (万) wàn n., ten thousand, myriad L6

曾 Zēng n., Zeng (family name [姓] of a disciple of Kǒngzǐ; 名 參。字子輿。) L7

富 fù n., wealth L7

貴 (贵) guì n., esteem L7

惡 (恶) wù t.v., to dislike, to hate L7

然 rán s.v., to be so, to be this L8; v., -ingly (follows a stative verb, converting it into an adverb) L11

惠 Huì, n., Hui (family name [姓] of a philosopher known for his clever arguments, 惠子 Huìzǐ, Master Hui; 名施。) L10

遊 L10

循 L10

勞 (劳) láo t.v., to belabor, to make work for L11

惻隱 (恻隐) cèyǐn n., sympathy, compassion L12

猶 yóu v., to be like, to be similar to L12 (notes)

喻 yù t.v., to understand L13

13

遠 or 遠 (远) yuán s.v., to be far L1

愛 (爱) ài t.v., to love L3

罪 zuì n., crime, fault L6

與 (与) yǔ conj., and (joins nouns) L7; yú g.p. (sentence-final interrogative) L8; yú g.p. (sentence-final exclamatory) L13

夢 (梦) mèng n., dream L11; t.v., to dream (that) L13

楹 yíng, n., pillar L11

14

齊 (齐) Qí n., Qi (name of a state in what is now 山東 Shāndōng Province) L2

對 (对) duì adv., respondingly, in response L2

誨 huì t.v., to teach someone about something L4

聞 (闻) wén t.v., to hear L9

實 (实) shí n., reality (as opposed to appearance or manifestation) L9

疑 yí t.v., to suspect that, to wonder whether L11

端 duān n. tip; n. sprout L12

盡 (尽) jìn adv., wholly, completely, fully L12

緒 xù n., tip, end point L12 (notes)

適 (适) shì t.v., to satisfy L13

15

樊 Fán n., Fan (family name [姓] of a disciple of Kongzi; 名須。字子遲。) L3

遲 (迟) Chí n., Chi (part of the style [字] of a disciple of Kongzi; 姓樊。名須。字子遲。) L3

樂 (乐) lè t.v., to delight in L3; yuè n., music L3 (grammar notes)

諸 zhū g.p. (equivalent to 之乎 zhī hū, ". . . it?") L5

毅 yì s.v., to be resolute L7

賤 (贱) jiàn n., low prestige, low social status L7

賜 (赐) Cì n., Ci (personal name [名] of a disciple of Kongzi; 姓端木。字子貢。) L8

德 dé n., Virtue, political charisma generated by a good character L9

請 L10

醉 zuì s.v., to be intoxicated (may indicate a variety of states in between being mildly tipsy and being thoroughly drunk) L11

16

謂 (谓) wèi t.v., to say something of someone or something L6

學 (学) xué s.v., to study, to learn L8

舉 (举) jǔ t.v., to lift L11

頭 (头) tóu n., head L11

頹 (颓) tuí s.v., to slump, to sprawl L11

17

雖 (虽) suī conj., although, even though L5

縲紲 (缧绁) léi xiè n., fetters, ropes for binding prisoners L6

濠 háo n., Hao (name of a river) L10

鯈 L10

霜 shuāng n., frost L11

孺子 rúzǐ n., baby; n., toddler L12

19

識 (识) zhì t.v., to remember L8

蘧蘧 qúqú s.v., to be sudden L13

20

覺 (觉) jué s.v., to be conscious L13

22

體 (体) tǐ n., Substance (technical term in Confucian metaphysics; roughly, the 體 is what something is in itself, while its 用 yòng, Function, is how it manifests itself in action; the eye is 體, seeing is its 用; water is 體, waves are its 用) L9